Close *Reading* 9-12

Comprehension, Interpretation and Language Activities

MARY M FIRTH

ANDREW G RALSTON

HODDER
GIBSON

PART OF HACHETTE LIVRE UK

The Publishers would like to thank the following for permission to reproduce copyright material:

Photo credits
Page 10 © Peter Skinner/Science Photo Library; page 19 © Andrew Cooper/Naturepl.com; page 74 © Eric Baccega/Naturepl.com; page 77 (left) © Topfoto/ImageWorks; page 77 (right) © Tom Stewart/Corbis; page 78 © Daniel J. Cox/Corbis; page 81 © Popperfoto/Alamy; page 85 © Richard Wareham Fotografie/Alamy; page 89 © D. Hurst/Alamy; page 90 © Popperfoto.com; page 96 © Justin Kase/ Alamy; page 98 © © Bob Torrez / Alamy; page 100 © William Whitehurst/Corbis; page 102 © C/B Productions/Corbis; page 103 © Paul Almasy/Corbis; page 106 © SIME/Corbis; page 111 © Marcelo Del Pozo/Reuters/Corbis; page 113 © Marcelo Del Pozo/Reuters/Corbis; page 120 © Peter Newark's Pictures; page 122 © Photo courtesy of Lloyd's List; page 132 © Bettmann/Corbis; page 133 © NASA GPN-2002-0000541; page 140 © NASA GPN-2000-0010771.

Acknowledgements
Cartoons by the Richard Duszczak Cartoon Studio Limited.

Artworks by Clive Spong/Linden Artists.

Extracts from 'The Hill of the Red Fox' Copyright © Allan Campbell McLean, reproduced by permission of A M Heath & Co. Ltd; 'Christopher Mouse' © William Wise, reproduced by permission of Bloomsbury Publishing; 'A Stranger Came Ashore' Copyright © Mollie Hunter, reproduced by permission of A M Heath & Co. Ltd on behalf of Mollie Hunter as well as the publisher Floris Books; 'Danny, the Champion of the World' © Roald Dahl, reproduced by permission of David Higham Associates; 'The Turbulent Term of Tyke Tiler' © Gene Kemp, reproduced by permission of Pollinger Limited and Gene Kemp; 'Double Act' by Jacqueline Wilson, published by Doubleday/Corgi Yearling. Reprinted by permission of The Random House Group Ltd.; 'Buddy' © Nigel Hinton, reproduced by permission of Orion Children's Books, a division of The Orion Publishing Group; 'Meet the Polar Bear' © Malcolm Perry (Hodder Wayland); 'Football, the Global Game' from *An International Soccer Star* by Ben Godsall Reprinted by permission of Harcourt Education; 'Tetra Pak' from *The Modern Industrial World: Sweden* © Bo Kaye Carlsson (Hodder Wayland); 'Teeth Braces' from *Medicine* by Paul Dowswell. Reprinted by permission of Harcourt Education; 'Tourism in Majorca' from *The Modern Industrial World: Spain* © Neil Champion (Hodder Wayland); 'The Highland Clearances' © Donald Gunn and Marie Spankie (Hodder Wayland); 'The Ship That Cried' (The Wreck of the Derbyshire) from *Shipping Disasters* by Rob Alcraft. Reprinted by permission of Harcourt Education; 'Apollo 13' from *Days That Shook the World: The Moon Landing* © Paul Mason (Hodder Wayland).

The authors would like to thank Diane Mitchell for her comments and suggestions.

Every effort has been made to trace all copyright holders, but if any have been inadvertently overlooked the Publishers will be pleased to make the necessary arrangements at the first opportunity.

Although every effort has been made to ensure that website addresses are correct a time of going to press, Hodder Gibson cannot be held responsible for the content of any website mentioned in this book. It is sometimes possible to find a relocated web page by typing in the address of the home page for a website in the URL window of your browser.

Papers used in this book are natural, renewable and recyclable products. They are made from wood grown in sustainable forests. The logging and manufacturing processes conform to the environmental regulations of the country of origin.

Orders: please contact Bookpoint Ltd, 130 Milton Park, Abingdon, Oxon OX14 4SB. Telephone: (44) 01235 827720. Fax: (44) 01235 400454. Lines are open from 9.00–5.00, Monday to Saturday, with a 24-hour message answering service. Visit our website at www.hoddereducation.co.uk. Hodder Gibson can be contacted direct on: Tel: 0141 848 1609; Fax: 0141 889 6315; email: hoddergibson@hodder.co.uk

© Mary M Firth and Andrew G Ralston 2006
First published in 2006 by
Hodder Gibson, an imprint of Hodder Education, part of Hachette Livre UK
2a Christie Street
Paisley PA1 1NB

Impression number   10 9 8 7 6 5 4 3
Year   2010 2009 2008

Cover illustrations by David Parkins
Typeset in Stane Sans 13pt by Fakenham Photosetting Limited, Norfolk.
Printed and bound in Great Britain by Martins The Printers, Berwick-upon-Tweed.

A catalogue record for this title is available from the British Library

ISBN-13: 978-0-340-91472-4

Contents

Introduction to the Teacher

This book is designed to provide Close Reading (comprehension) practice for pupils in upper primary years.

The book will be particularly suitable for pupils who are being entered for National Tests at Level D. As in the test papers, both narrative and factual (reading for information) passages are provided. The question types, such as 'true/false/can't tell' and 'underline the most suitable ending', are similar to those in the test papers.

In addition to providing practice for National Tests, the book aims to introduce primary pupils to the skills required for Close Reading in the secondary school. A key aspect is the ability to answer in the pupil's own words, and questions of this type are included alongside ones that simply require the pupil to find a quotation or single word from the text.

As most schools already have suitable programmes for the teaching of basic grammar, it is not the purpose of the book to go over this ground in depth. (Grammar is covered in the *Knowledge about Language* textbook first published in 1996 and revised in 2000 (ISBN: 07169 60168)). However, each passage has some follow-up exercises giving practice in particular language skills that will assist pupils with Close Reading work and National Tests. Many of the aspects of language work mentioned in *English Language 5 – 14: Curriculum and Assessment in Scotland National Guidelines* as being appropriate to Level D are referred to – including punctuation, paragraphing, dictionary work, fact/opinion, points of view and the differences between dialect and Standard English.

The *Guidelines* encourage the use of Scottish material and this emphasis was borne in mind in selecting suitable passages. In addition, each chapter concludes with suggestions for the pupils' own writing, stimulated by ideas and topics in the passages.

Since classroom resources do not always permit answer sheets to be used on a once-only basis, this book contains questions in a format which will allow pupils to answer on paper or in their own work-

books. This will enable the books to be recycled for future year groups.

The teacher's book which accompanies this volume contains photocopiable answer sheets on which pupils can write their answers directly, using techniques such as underlining, ticking boxes, or filling in gaps. The format is similar to that used in the National Tests and will enable pupils to complete the tests more quickly. Teachers can use these sheets to practise for the National Tests. The teacher's book also contains marking schemes.

MMF/AGR

Starting Close Reading

William and Hannah were not sure about doing Close Reading tests. They asked their teacher, Miss Jolly, to help . . .

'Close Reading' – what is that?

CLOSE READING!

'Close Reading' is when you read a short piece of writing very carefully and then answer questions on it.

Why? I like reading, but answering questions seems like work! I would rather read more of the story!

This is an important skill for life. If you get a new mobile phone, for example, you have to be able to follow the instructions.

Well, one reason is that the questions help you think carefully about what the writer says, instead of just skimming over the words.

Also, the questions will give you practice in the English tests you will have to do in the future.

OSE
ADING!

But what if I get the answers wrong? I'm feeling nervous now!

Don't worry! If you get some answers wrong in one test, your teacher will help you with the bits you are finding difficult. Practising doing the tests really helps – you will soon get used to the kind of questions they ask.

What kind of questions will be in the tests?

CLOSE

READING!

There are several different types. In one type, you will be asked to choose the best ending to a sentence about the text – the 'text' is the story. You will get three endings to choose from.

For example, if one sentence began, 'Hannah and William were asking their teacher...', which of these endings would you choose?

a) what their Close Reading book was about
b) what she would like for her birthday
c) when it would be lunch time

That's too easy! The answer is a).

Yes, that was very easy. But it is an example which shows you how to answer that type of question. All you need to do is write down the letter, or sometimes you might be asked to underline the right answer.

Will any of the questions ask about language or style – how the story is written? What will we have to know?

Yes, some of the questions will ask about language, and there are a few things you will be expected to know. Why don't we take a minute to look at these?

For practice (1)

Here is the list Miss Jolly gave to William and Hannah. Check how many of these language terms you know. For each term, write down what it means, and then give two examples of your own. One or two answers are already filled in to start you off. A neat way to do this exercise is to copy out the table and fill in your answers. Be sure to make your boxes big enough to write in!

Term	Meaning of Term	Examples
1 **Noun**		1 2
2 **Verb**	A 'doing' word	1 2
3 **Adjective**		1 2
4 **Adverb**		1 quickly 2
5 **Sentence**		1 2
6 **Phrase**		1 2
7 **Simile**		1 2

Tell us more about the kinds of questions we will get in the tests.

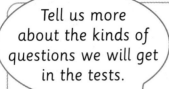

Another type of question is where you are asked to say if something is 'false' 'true' or 'can't tell'. For example, if the sentence was, 'Miss Jolly is a teacher', the answer would be 'true'.

Or, if the sentence was, 'Miss Jolly has two heads', then it would be 'false'. But if it was, 'Miss Jolly has two sisters' you would have to say 'can't tell' because you don't know if I have or not!

I like doing 'true or false' questions since you don't need to write very much! What other questions are there?

There is often a summary with blanks to fill in. A summary is a short simple version of the whole text. You'll be asked to fill one or two words into each blank space.

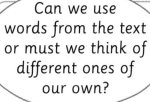

Can we use words from the text or must we think of different ones of our own?

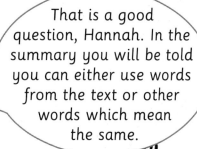

That is a good question, Hannah. In the summary you will be told you can either use words from the text or other words which mean the same.

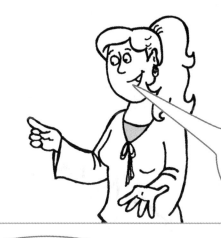

But there will often be one or two questions which tell you to 'Use your own words'. Then you *must* use different words in your answer as far as possible – of course you may repeat common words like 'and'!

Why do we have to 'use our own words'? Why can't we just pick out words from the story?

It's to show that you really understand the question, and that you don't just get the answer right by good luck! I'd like you to try this exercise which will give you some practice in 'using your own words'. I don't think you will find it difficult.

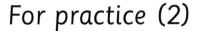

For practice (2)

It is possible to express the same idea in several different ways.

For example, instead of saying,

> 'The meal was delicious.'

you could say . . .

> 'The food tasted good.'

Rewrite these sentences, using your own words instead of the underlined ones, so that your new sentence still gives the same meaning. You may change around other parts of the sentence as well, if you wish, but you must keep the meaning the same.

1 Sally was <u>delighted</u> when she <u>came first in</u> her race.

2 Simon was <u>talented</u> at maths, but he <u>enjoyed</u> reading more.

3 An <u>elderly</u> <u>lady</u> was sitting on the <u>bench</u>.

4 I <u>believe</u> that Stephen sometimes <u>is</u> <u>untruthful</u>.

5 I shall try to <u>find out</u> what his friend <u>is called</u>.

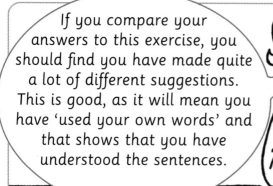

If you compare your answers to this exercise, you should find you have made quite a lot of different suggestions. This is good, as it will mean you have 'used your own words' and that shows that you have understood the sentences.

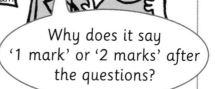

Why does it say '1 mark' or '2 marks' after the questions?

Most of the questions in the tests are worth 1 mark. However, if a question has more than one part – for example, if you are asked to 'Find two words' – you will get one mark for each, giving a total of 2 marks for the question.

It is important to notice the number of marks so that you don't miss out part of the answer.

I don't feel so nervous, now. But I still like reading the stories better than doing the questions!

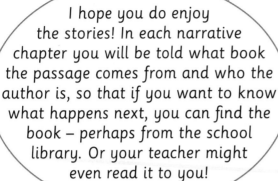

Chapter 1

The Hill of the Red Fox

Allan Campbell McLean's adventure story begins with Alasdair Cameron being sent from his home in London to stay with his Uncle Murdo Beaton on the Isle of Skye.

On the train journey north, someone passes Alasdair a strange note that reads 'Hunt at the Hill of the Red Fox M15'. When he arrives on the island he soon finds he has become mixed up in some sinister and dangerous goings-on . . .

Reading extract

1   Aunt Evelyn saw us off at Euston Station on a sunny
Monday morning. In the dim cavern of the station all
was bustle and movement. Porters rushed here and
there with trucks piled high with baggage; long queues
5   formed outside the ticket offices, and latecomers
hurried for their trains. At regular intervals a voice
blared over the loudspeakers announcing train
departures.

    'Attention, please,' boomed the voice. 'The eight-
10   thirty to Glasgow will be leaving Platform Twelve in
five minutes' time, calling at Rugby, Stafford, Crewe,
Carlisle . . .'

    'Oh, hurry,' I urged, one eye on the large black
minute-hand of the station clock, slowly creeping
15   round to the half-hour mark, 'or we will miss the train.'

Reading extract continued

Aunt Evelyn was calmly selecting magazines at the bookstall, and all she said was: 'Don't fuss so, Alasdair. I have never yet missed a train, and I do so hate spending hours over farewells.'

20 She collected several magazines and paid the girl, then added in a kindlier tone, doubtless conscious of my squirming impatience: 'Don't worry, I promise you we shan't miss the train.'

Aunt Evelyn was as good as her word. She found us 25 two corner seats, settled our luggage on the rack to her own satisfaction, and kissed my mother good-bye before the guard's whistle shrilled.

She shook hands with me through the open window and when I withdrew my hand I discovered a ten 30 pound note in my palm. I blurted out my thanks, but the train was already moving slowly out of the station, and I doubt if Aunt Evelyn heard me. But she smiled and waved, and I felt, without knowing why, that she

Reading extract continued

35 was pleased with me, and the realisation of this was so
unexpected that I wanted to cry out to her that I was
sorry for all the things that I had said and done in the
past. But such thoughts always come too late, and, as if
to make up for all that I had left unsaid, I waved and
waved until she was a tiny speck in the distance.

40   I hardly remember anything about the journey to
Glasgow, although most of the time I gazed out of the
window watching the green fields go spinning by. My
mother never spoke, except to answer my questions,
but from time to time I felt her eyes on me. Whenever I
45 looked up she smiled and went on with her reading,
but I knew that something was troubling her. I could
not understand why she could not accept my holiday
in Skye in the same happy spirit as Aunt Evelyn had
shown. But such dismal thoughts were soon forgotten
50 in the growing excitement of the journey ahead. In a
few hours we would be in Glasgow, and the very next
morning I would be starting out on my own, like any
lone adventurer from a tale of long ago.

Questions

*Lines 1–39 of the passage describe the station before the train
sets off on its journey north.*

1 The writer compares the station to 'a dim cavern'
(line 2).

Write down **TWO** words from this list which fit this description of the station.

> bright   small   dark   large
> underground   cramped

(2 marks)

2 'In the station all was bustle and movement' (lines 2–3). From the first paragraph, write down **TWO** examples of how busy and active people in the station were. *(2 marks)*

3 a)   Find **TWO** separate verbs from lines 6–12 which show that the station announcements were very loud. *(2 marks)*

   b)   Find **ONE** word in paragraph four (lines 16–19) which describes how Aunt Evelyn was acting at this point in the story. *(1 mark)*

   c)   Copy a phrase from paragraph five (lines 20–23) which describes Alasdair's feelings at the time. *(1 mark)*

4 Look at lines 24–27. Write down **TWO** helpful things that Aunt Evelyn did when the travellers got onto the train. *(2 marks)*

5 What action shows that Aunt Evelyn was a generous person? *(1 mark)*

6 'I blurted out my thanks' (line 30). Which of the following words best describes how Alasdair felt at this stage of the story?
   A   annoyed
   B   embarrassed
   C   excited *(1 mark)*

Lines 40–53 describe the train journey from London to Glasgow.

7 Decide whether each of these sentences is **true** or **false** or whether you **can't tell** from the passage. Copy this table into your book and complete it.

	true	false	can't tell
a) Alasdair was going to Skye on holiday.			
b) Alasdair's mother was happy about his trip to Skye.			
c) Aunt Evelyn was very fond of going to Skye herself.			
d) Alasdair would not arrive in Skye the same day.			

(4 marks)

8 a) Find an example of a simile in the last paragraph of the passage. *(1 mark)*

b) What does this expression tell us about how Alasdair felt about the next stage of his journey? *(2 marks)*

9 Complete these sentences by choosing the best ending.

a) When Alasdair heard the train was leaving in five minutes, he:
   A rushed on board
   B tried to get his aunt to hurry up
   C went to choose a magazine *(1 mark)*

b) Aunt Evelyn wasn't rushing, even though the train was due to leave in five minutes. This was because:
   A she didn't realise the train was due to leave
   B she wanted to say goodbye quickly
   C she was more interested in choosing a magazine *(1 mark)*

c) 'Aunt Evelyn was as good as her word' (line 24) means:

   A Aunt Evelyn did what she said she would

   B she spoke in a kindly manner

   C she was interesting to talk to   *(1 mark)*

d) Alasdair wanted to say sorry to Aunt Evelyn because:

   A he had not thanked her properly for giving him money

   B he was leaving her to go on a journey

   C he was sorry for things he had said and done in the past   *(1 mark)*

e) Alasdair was travelling on the train journey:

   A by himself

   B with his Aunt Evelyn

   C with his mother   *(1 mark)*

f) During the journey to Glasgow Alasdair spent most of the time:

   A reading a book

   B looking out of the window

   C planning what he would do when he reached his destination.   *(1 mark)*

Total – 25 marks

Taking a closer look

Sentences (1)

To make sense of words, we have to group them into sentences.

There are four main things that make a group of words a sentence:

For example,

> **Aunt Evelyn saw us off at Euston Station on a sunny Monday morning.**

is a sentence but

> **In the dim cavern of the station.**

is not. Why?

For practice

Decide whether each of the following is a sentence or not.

1 He shook hands with me.

2 I blurted out my thanks.

3 All the things I had said and done in the past.

4 The train was moving slowly out of the station.

5 The journey to Glasgow.

6 Whenever I looked up.

7 I knew that something was troubling her.

8 To answer my questions.

9 Most of the time.

10 The very next morning I would be starting out on my own.

Follow on

Topics for discussion

1 Write down three reasons why you would like to read more of this story. Discuss your reasons with your class or group.

2 Discuss the ways in which travelling by train can be more or less enjoyable than other forms of transport, such as car, bus or plane.

Writing

1 Think about what might happen next in the story. Why is Alasdair's mother troubled? Do you think Alasdair will enjoy the holiday as much as he thinks? Write a few more pages of this story, describing what happens after Alasdair arrives in Glasgow.

Follow on continued

2 *'The Journey of a Lifetime'*

Write an account of a journey you yourself have been on. Was it enjoyable and exciting, or was it one of these trips where everything went wrong?

Chapter 2

Christopher Mouse

This extract from **Christopher Mouse: the Tale of a Small Traveller**, a novel by William Wise, describes the first few weeks of Christopher's life, and his first impressions of Mrs Crimmins who brings him his food.

Reading extract

1 My life began in the most commonplace way. I was born

5 in an ordinary wire cage, on a soft bed of paper shavings. A few pieces of lettuce

10 and a few lumps of cheese were strewn here and there.

At first my eyes remained shut so that I could not see anything around me. I slept most of the time, for I was very weak. I remember wondering why there was a

15 rustling sound whenever I moved. But before long I grew so tired thinking about it that I feel asleep again.

Finally the day came when I was able to open my eyes. I saw the cage where I was lying and climbed unsteadily to my feet. Step by step I began to explore. I

20 nosed around among the papers; I sampled the lettuce
and the cheese; I drank from the round saucer that
stood in the corner. The surface of the water cast a
reflection. In it, I saw myself for the first time – my
eyes, my nose, my fur and my whiskers.

25   Then, one after another, I met four beings who
looked like my own image in the water. They were my
three brothers and my sister, Anna. She was smaller
than they were, and from the beginning I knew I liked
her best.

30   When my mother saw that I was up and about, she
began to explain things to me. 'You are a white mouse
like the rest of us,' she told me, 'and you will live in
this cage for six or seven weeks – until Mrs Crimmins
comes to fetch you.'

35   'Who is Mrs Crimmins?' I asked her.

'She is the woman who owns us,' my mother said.
'In fact, she owns everything in this room – the food
we eat, the cage we live in – everything.'

'Do you like Mrs Crimmins?' I asked.

40   My mother did not reply at once. She frowned and
twitched her whiskers reflectively for several moments,
and then I heard her sigh. 'I suppose I like her well
enough,' she told me. 'She *might* treat us worse than
she does. Some owners are good – though I suspect not

45 many of them – and some owners are wicked. I imagine
– but I can't be sure – that Mrs Crimmins falls
somewhere in between.'

Before I could ask her anything more, I heard a noise
behind me. When I turned, I saw that a stout woman

Reading extract continued

50 with bright red hair had come into the room. Mother told me it was Mrs Crimmins, bringing us our food.

I'll never forget the first time she opened our cage to feed us. There was a long trapdoor at the top of the cage. She slid it back, and as she did, I heard a terrible

55 grating sound that made the fur along my spine stand on end.

Her fingers appeared at the opening. They held strips of bruised lettuce and bits of yellow, mouldy cheese. She dropped them into our cage, wriggling those fat

60 fingers above our heads like five pale sausages. They were not a pretty sight to see.

Having given us the lettuce and cheese, she dropped in our weekly treat – six well-salted mixed nuts. And they really were a treat for us. Many people think we

65 dote on cheese, that it's our favourite food, but this simply is not true. Give any mouse a pecan or a walnut, an almond or a cashew, and he'll be extremely grateful. All mice have a passion for nuts, and that's the way to charm us if you should ever wish to.

70 I didn't know what to make of Mrs Crimmins after that. Certainly the food she fed us most of the time was nothing to boast of – especially the cheese, which must have been considerably older than I was myself. And yet, she was not entirely devoid of kindness, for she

75 also provided us with a weekly treat of salted nuts. Was she good – or was she not? I began to see why my mother had answered me so vaguely.

Questions

Section A

Complete these sentences by choosing the best ending.

1 The mouse could not see things around him because:
   A his eyes had not yet opened
   B he was asleep at the time
   C he was unwell

2 When Christopher asks 'Do you like Mrs Crimmins?' his mother does not reply at once because:
   A she did not like the question
   B she was fed up with being asked questions
   C she was not sure how to answer

3 Christopher's mother felt that:
   A only a few people were good to mice
   B most people were good to mice
   C Mrs Crimmins treated them very well

4 When Mrs Crimmins opened the trapdoor to feed the mice, Christopher felt frightened because:
   A he did not like the food
   B he did not like the noise made by the door
   C he did not like Mrs Crimmins

5 'She was not entirely devoid of kindness' (line 74) means:
   A she never showed any affection towards the mice
   B she always showed them affection
   C she only showed them affection on some occasions

(5 marks)

Section B

Lines 1–29 describe the early stages of Christopher's life.

1 Find another word in this section of the passage which is similar in meaning to 'commonplace' (line 3). *(1 mark)*

2 'Step by step I began to explore' (line 19). **In your own words**, explain **TWO** of the things Christopher did.

(2 marks)

3 Explain how Christopher learns what he looks like.

(1 mark)

4 'From the beginning I liked her best' (lines 28–29). Why do you think he liked his sister Anna more than his brothers? *(1 mark)*

5 What does Christopher's mother thinks will happen to him in the future? *(1 mark)*

Lines 30–47 describe how Christopher's mother feels about their owner, Mrs Crimmins.

6 a) Write down **TWO** expressions which show that his mother was unsure about her feelings towards Mrs Crimmins. *(2 marks)*

b) Explain why so many dashes are used in lines 44–47.

(1 mark)

Lines 48–77 describe Mrs Crimmins and how she treats the mice.

7 **In your own words** describe **ONE** feature of Mrs Crimmins' appearance. *(1 mark)*

8 Write down the words that tell the reader the effect the noise of the trapdoor had on Christopher. *(1 mark)*

9 **In your own words**, describe the kind of food that Mrs Crimmins gave the mice. *(2 marks)*

10 What **TWO** things do we learn about the kind of food that mice like to eat? *(2 marks)*

11 In lines 75–76 Christopher asks himself: 'Was she good –
or was she not?' Write down **ONE** piece of evidence
from the passage that suggests Mrs Crimmins was
'good' and **ONE** piece of evidence that suggests she
was not.   *(2 marks)*

Section C

Complete these sentences by choosing the best ending.

1 The word 'strewn' (line 11) means:
   A   scattered about
   B   placed
   C   spread out

2 The word 'grating' (line 55) means:
   A   growling
   B   scraping
   C   roaring

3 Find a word from the last paragraph which means 'in a
   way that is not very clear or distinct'.   *(3 marks)*

Total – 25 marks

Taking a closer look

Sentences (2)

In the last chapter, we looked at what a sentence was. Can
you remember the four things that can be said about any
sentence?

Here is the next part of the story of Christopher Mouse.
Unfortunately, one of the mice has nibbled away at the

passage and all the full stops are missing! Rewrite it, with the proper punctuation.

One day I decided I must know the answer I came to my mother she was sitting in a corner I said, 'You told me once that I would live here six or seven weeks after that Mrs Crimmins would come to fetch me what did you mean when you said that why will she come to fetch me' I saw a startled look in my mother's eyes a grave expression stole across her face she pretended to be unconcerned but my question had pained her I had never seen her upset before suddenly I felt a pang of fear my sister, Anna, and my three brothers must have felt the same anxiety they began to crowd around me

Hint

There should be **FOURTEEN** different sentences here. Twelve of them should end with a full stop and the other two should end with question marks.

Follow on

Topics for discussion

1 Write down three reasons why you would like to read more of this story. Discuss your reasons with your class or group.

2 Do you have a pet? Talk to your group or class about the problems and pleasures of looking after a pet.

Writing

1 Imagine that you are an animal. Write about a day in your life.

OR

2 Write a few pages of your own life story, starting with your very first memories.

Chapter 3

A Stranger Came Ashore

A Stranger Came Ashore by Mollie Hunter is set in Shetland. The main character is a ten-year-old boy called Robbie Henderson. Shetland has many legends about seals, or 'selkies', which are said to take human form, and sometimes cause harm to people. Robbie has always wanted to touch a seal, and here he has taken his father's rowing boat out to search for baby seals, known as 'pups'. At last he finds a group unguarded in a little bay.

Reading extract

1 Eight white seal pups lay on the tiny beach. There was no sign of the bull seal which usually lay roaring there – no sign even of a single cow seal. With his heart hammering out a great drumbeat on his ribs, Robbie let
5 the boat ground gently on the shingle. Stepping knee-deep into the water, he edged the prow on to the stones. Then, moving as silently and cautiously as possible, he approached the nearest of the pups and knelt beside it. Gently he reached out a hand, and laid
10 it on the thick, white fur.

The pup's great, round eyelids snapped open. Its mouth opened also, showing two rows of very white, very sharp teeth. Rolling quickly over on to its belly, it made an angry hissing noise at Robbie. Then, with strong, rapid

Reading extract continued

15 movements of its flippers, it began pulling itself away from
him. Robbie stared after it, swallowing his disappointment
as best he could before he turned to the next pup.

This one was also lying on its back, and it seemed
even more sound asleep than the first pup had been,
20 for it hardly stirred at all when Robbie ventured a
gentle hand on its fur. Cautiously he knelt beside it.
With his right hand supporting himself on the shingle,
he let his left hand travel slowly, very slowly, across the
pup's soft, wet fur. And slowly, slowly, as Robbie's
25 fingers caressed it, the pup awakened.

It stretched, tail and flippers quivering. It made little,
contented mewing noises, and its head rolled round to
rest against Robbie's right forearm. Its eyes opened;
great, dark brown shining eyes as round as buttons,
30 that stared soulfully up at him.

Robbie began to tremble with the effort not to
laugh at this look. The pup was still leaning its head

Reading extract continued

against his right arm, and when he thought he had
control of himself, he slipped his left arm around the
35 other side of its body. Carefully then he gathered the
pup clear of the shingle; and rose, holding it cradled in
his arms.

It was astonishingly heavy, he found, for such a
young creature. And even more astonishing was the
40 heat that came from its damp little body. Holding it,
thought Robbie, was like holding a little furnace against
his chest.

The black nails on the underside of the pup's flippers
caught his attention, and he put one finger against
45 them to see what it would do. Immediately it bent its
flipper so that it could grip the finger with these nails,
and there was such strength in the grip that Robbie
realised there was no way of breaking it except by
laying the pup down. Unwillingly, he did so, and then
50 saw the reason for the power of the pup's grip as it bent
its flippers again and used the nails to pull itself rapidly
away over the shingle.

The other pups on the beach were all awake, their
heads turning towards him, their bright, brown-button
55 eyes staring. Robbie approached them one by one,
stepping gently, going down on one knee beside them;
but the pups would have none of him. They hissed,
showing rows of sharp white teeth as the first pup had
done. Even the pup he had lifted was unfriendly, now
60 that it was wide awake, and could sense the alarm of
the others; and resigning himself to this at last, Robbie
walked back to the boat.

Reading extract continued

But still, he told himself, he had done what he had set out to do. He had discovered at last what it *felt* like
65 to hold a selkie, and so he had learned something that even his old grandfather had never been able to teach him – quite apart from which, it had been fun to hold the pup!

Questions

In the first part of the passage (lines 1–17), Robbie approaches the seal pups.

1 Complete these sentences by choosing the best ending.

a) The eight seal pups were on the beach:
   A with a roaring bull seal
   B by themselves
   C with a single cow seal

b) Robbie knelt down by the first pup:
   A and touched it gently
   B and tried to pick it up
   C but did not touch it

c) The pup woke up and:
   A moved towards him
   B moved into the water
   C moved away from him

(3 marks)

2 a) Did the pup open its eyes quickly or slowly? *(1 mark)*

b) Write down the word which helped you to find the answer to 2 a). *(1 mark)*

3 a) Write down a single word from paragraph 2 (lines 11–17) which tells of the seal pup's mood. *(1 mark)*

b) In your own words, explain **ONE** action of the seal which shows this mood. *(1 mark)*

4 Write down the word which shows how Robbie feels when he fails to lift this pup. *(1 mark)*

In the second part of the passage (lines 18–42), Robbie succeeds in picking up a seal pup.

5 From the third paragraph (lines 18–25), find **ONE** word that means the same as each of these words or expressions:

> moved   risked   pebbly beach   stroked

(4 marks)

6 Explain in your own words what the seal pup did that made Robbie want to laugh. *(1 mark)*

7 What was the **first** thing that Robbie thought was astonishing when he picked up the seal? *(1 mark)*

8 The second thing he noticed that was even more astonishing was that the pup felt very warm. Write down the **simile** from paragraph 6 (lines 38–42) which makes this clear. *(1 mark)*

In the last part of the passage (lines 43–68), Robbie lets the seal pup go.

9 Look at these sentences about the last part of the passage. Decide whether each sentence is **true** or **false** or whether you **can't tell** from the passage. Copy this table into your exercise book and complete it.

	true	false	can't tell
a) The strong grip of the seal helps it move quickly along the ground.			
b) The pup Robbie had held was not so unfriendly as the others.			
c) Seal pups are more nervous of humans than adult seals are.			

(3 marks)

10 Here is a summary of the passage. Suggest **one word or two words** to fill each space. You may use your own word or words from the passage. Write your answers in a list, using the numbers given with each space.

Robbie found eight seal pups lying on a ____1____. He approached the pups, moving ____2____ so that he would not disturb them. When he reached the first pup, it snapped open its eyes and ____3____ at Robbie, before moving quickly away. The second pup Robbie touched woke up ____4____. It then ____5____ at him with its big eyes. This made Robbie want to ____6____. Since it did not seem ____7____, Robbie lifted it up. He was astonished at how ____8____ and ____9____ it was. When Robbie put a finger against its flipper, it ____10____ him with its ____11____, and Robbie had to set the seal down again to release his finger. However, Robbie felt ____12____ because he had now held a 'selkie'.

(12 marks)

Total – 30 marks

Taking a closer look

Point of View

When telling a story, an author may write as if it is one of the characters who is telling the story. The story will use words like 'I', 'me' and 'myself'. This is known as writing '**in the first person**'.

On the other hand, the author may choose to write '**in the third person**'. *A Stranger Came Ashore* contains a character called Robbie Henderson. The author calls the character 'Robbie' and speaks about him as 'he'.

In *A Stranger Came Ashore,* the author makes Robbie the central character, and always tells the reader what Robbie is thinking and doing.

For practice (1)

Rewrite the last paragraph of the extract, changing it from **third person** to **first person**. The first few words are done for you to start you off.

Extract in the third person
'But still, he told himself, he had done what he had set out to do. He had discovered at last what it *felt* like to hold a selkie, and so he had learned something that even his old grandfather had never been able to teach him.'

First person version
'But still, I told myself, I had done what . . .'

For practice (2)

1 Rewrite the following sentences in the **first person**, as if you are the person named in brackets:

a) Michael told his teacher that he had lost his homework. (Michael)

b) Sara's mother drops her off at school on her way to work. (Sara)

c) Mark was shocked to see his brother smoking on their school bus. (Mark)

2 Rewrite the following sentences in the **third person**. (The name of the speaker or speakers is in brackets):

a) We always go to Spain for our summer holidays. (David and Anne)

b) I want to be a vet when I grow up. (Linda)

c) Luckily I was not hurt when I fell off my skateboard. (Martin)

Follow on

Topics for discussion

In the story, Robbie's ambition was to hold a seal pup and he was very pleased when he achieved this. What would you specially like to do? In your class or group, explain what you would most like to do and why.

Follow on continued

Writing

1 Write about an interesting or unusual experience you have had.

2 Write a story in which a boy or girl has an encounter with an animal.

Chapter 4

Danny, the Champion of the World

In this story by Roald Dahl, Danny is an eight-year old boy who lives alone with his father in a caravan behind the garage where his father works. Although Danny's mother died when he was just a baby, Danny is very happy with his life.

Reading extract

1   And so life went on. The world I lived in consisted only of the filling-station, the workshop, the caravan, the school, and of course the woods and fields and streams in the countryside around. But I was never bored. It

5   was impossible to be bored in my father's company. He was too sparky a man for that. Plots and plans and new ideas came flying off him like sparks from a **grindstone**.

> *Note*
>
> **grindstone:** *stone for sharpening metal tools*

27

Reading extract continued

'There's a good wind today,' he said one Saturday
morning. 'Just right for flying a kite. Let's make a kite,
10 Danny.'

So we made a kite. He showed me how to splice four
thin sticks together in the shape of a star, with two
more sticks across the middle to brace it. Then we cut
up an old blue shirt of his and stretched the material
15 across the frame-work of the kite. We added a long tail
made of thread, with little leftover pieces of the shirt
tied at intervals along it. We found a ball of string in
the workshop and he showed me how to attach the
string to the framework so that the kite would be
20 properly balanced in flight.

Together we walked to the top of the hill behind the
filling-station to release the kite. I found it hard to
believe that this object, made only from a few sticks
and a piece of old shirt, would actually fly. I held the
25 string while my father held the kite, and the moment
he let it go, it caught the wind and soared upward like
a huge blue bird.

'Let out some more, Danny!' he cried. 'Go on! As
much as you like!'

30 Higher and higher soared the kite. Soon it was just a
small blue dot dancing in the sky miles above my head,
and it was thrilling to stand there holding on to
something that was so far away and so very much alive.
This faraway thing was tugging and struggling on the
35 end of the line like a big fish.

'Let's walk it back to the caravan,' my father said.
So we walked down the hill again with me holding the ➤

Reading extract continued

string and the kite pulling fiercely on the other end. When we came to the caravan we were careful not to get the string tangled in the apple tree and we brought it all the way round to the front steps.

'Tie it up to the steps,' my father said.

'Will it stay up?' I asked.

'It will if the wind doesn't drop,' he said.

The wind didn't drop. And I will tell you something amazing. That kite stayed up there all through the night, and at breakfast time next morning the small blue dot was still dancing and swooping in the sky. After breakfast I hauled it down and hung it carefully against a wall in the workshop for another day.

'You can fly the kite all by yourself any time you like,' my father said.

So you can see that being eight years old and living with my father was a lot of fun. But I was impatient to be nine. I reckoned that being nine would be even more fun than being eight.

Questions

Section A

In the first paragraph of the passage, Danny talks about his life with his father.

1 Write down a phrase from the first paragraph which shows how interesting Danny finds his life. *(1 mark)*

2 Danny describes his father as 'sparky'. Which **ONE** of the following words do you think is closest in meaning to this?

bad-tempered   lively   thoughtful   talkative

(1 mark)

3 'like sparks from a grindstone' (line 7)

Which **ONE** of the following best describes the effect of this expression?

a) the ideas were dangerous like the hot flying sparks

b) the ideas were exciting and there were lots of them like the bright sparks

c) the ideas would just die away like the sparks

Choose a), b) or c) for your answer.   *(1 mark)*

In the next part of the passage (lines 11–20), Danny describes making the kite.

4 What gave Danny's father the idea for making a kite that day?   *(1 mark)*

5 Find words from the third paragraph (lines 11–20) which mean the same as the following:

a) join

b) strengthen.   *(2 marks)*

In the third part of the passage (lines 21–35), Danny actually flies the kite.

6 Write down the **simile** from the fourth paragraph (lines 21–27) which describes the kite flying.   *(1 mark)*

7 Danny says the kite seemed to be 'miles above' his head (line 31).

Write down a phrase from paragraph 6 (lines 30–35) which shows the kite was so high it could hardly be seen. *(1 mark)*

8 a) Write down a word from paragraph 6 which describes how Danny feels when he flies the kite.

(1 mark)

b) Suggest **a word of your own** which means the same as your answer to question 8a). *(1 mark)*

9 Danny says the way the kite pulls on the string makes it feel as if it is 'alive'.

a) Write down a **simile** from paragraph 6 which shows it feels as if it is alive. *(1 mark)*

b) From the same paragraph, write down **TWO** words ending with '**_ing**' which also suggest the kite is alive. *(2 marks)*

In the last part of the passage (lines 36–56), Danny takes the kite home.

10 In lines 45–46, Danny says 'I will tell you something amazing'.

In your own words, explain what the 'amazing thing' was. *(1 mark)*

11 It is clear that Danny intended to fly the kite again. Explain how the reader can tell this from information in lines 45–50) *(1 mark)*

Section B

Look at these sentences about the passage. Decide whether each sentence is **true** or **false** or whether you **can't tell** from the passage. Copy this table into your exercise book and complete it.

	true	false	can't tell
a) Danny did not have anyone to play with except his father.			
b) Danny's father was very good at making things with his hands.			
c) The hill behind the filling-station was a popular place for flying kites.			
d) It took a little time to get the kite to fly up high.			
e) Danny's father was happy to let Danny play without supervision.			

(5 marks)

Section C

Complete these sentences by choosing the best ending.

1 The main reason Danny enjoyed his life was because:
  A he was allowed to help in the filling-station and the workshop
  B he enjoyed exploring the countryside
  C his father was always thinking up interesting things to do

2 Making the kite was as much fun as flying it because:
  A Danny's father let Danny help and showed him what to do

    B Danny enjoyed watching his father since he was such
an expert

    C the materials they used to make it were so interesting

3 Danny did not expect the kite to fly well because:
    A they had never made a kite before
    B it was made of very cheap simple materials
    C he knew it was difficult to get kites off the ground

4 In lines 28–29, the writer uses many exclamation marks:

'Let out some more, Danny!' he cried. 'Go on! As much
as you like!'

This is to show
    A Danny's father is shouting very loudly at Danny
    B Danny's father is getting impatient with Danny
    C Danny's father is also very excited about flying the kite

5 Danny was looking forward to being nine because:
    A he enjoyed being eight so much he was sure nine
would be even better
    B there were many things he could not do when he
was only eight
    C his father would let him do more things by himself
when he was nine

(5 marks)

Total – 25 marks

Taking a closer look

Sentences (3)

You have already learned that a sentence is a group of words
which makes sense by itself and that every sentence starts
with a **capital** letter.

There are three main types of sentence:

* A **statement** tells you something: *The kite flew up in the air.* It ends with a **full stop**.

* A **question** asks you something: *Will the kite fly?* It ends with a **question mark**.

* A **command** tells you to do something: *Hold the string, please!* A command may end with an **exclamation mark**, or it may also end with a **full stop**.

For practice (1)

Look at these examples from the passage. Decide if each one is a statement, a question or a command.

1 'There's a good wind today,' he said.

2 Let out some more, Danny!

3 Tie it up to the steps.

4 Will it stay up?

For practice (2)

Decide if each of the following sentences is a statement, a question or a command. Then write out the sentence and put the correct punctuation mark after it. If the sentence is a command, you can decide if you think a full stop or an exclamation mark seems more suitable.

1 Danny lived with his father behind a garage

2 Do you think Danny had a nice life

3   Fetch the ball of string from the work-shop

4   Don't let it blow away

5   What colour was Danny's kite

Follow on

Topics for discussion

In the story, Danny has a very good relationship with his father.

1   Looking back at the story, explain why you think Danny and his father get on so well. Think of what Danny's father does for Danny and how he speaks to him and also how Danny behaves with his father.

2   From your own knowledge, discuss what you think makes 'a good Dad' or 'a good Mum'. Also, think of what makes someone 'a good son' or 'a good daughter'.

Writing

1   In the story, Danny tells about the fun he had flying his first kite. Write about an activity which you enjoy very much.

OR

2   Make up a story of your own about Danny and his father.

Chapter 5

The Turbulent Term of Tyke Tiler

In this extract from 'The Turbulent Term of Tyke Tiler' by
Gene Kemp, Tyke's class are told they are going to have
a student teacher. However, she turns out to be rather
different from what they expected . . .

Reading extract

1   'I want to tell you that the student we are having for
the next five weeks will be coming in this afternoon to
get to know you,' said the teacher.
    A terrible groan went up, because we'd already seen her.
5   ''er's 'orrible,' moaned Pitthead. He put his head on
the desk and made sick noises.
    'That's enough. Be fair and give her a chance.'
    'Pitthead's right. She looked at us as if we was dirt.'
    'Thank you for your opinion, Tyke. Shall we get on
10 with some work, now?'
    'We'd rather have you, Sir.'
    'I shall still have some lessons with you.'
    'Not enough. Why we gotter 'ave students?'
    'They 'ave to learn, don't they?'
15 'Not wiv us, they don't.'
    'They can't keep us quiet and then WE get into
trouble . . .'
    Sir exploded like a volcano and we got out our
folders in silence.

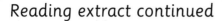

20   We came shouting and shoving into the classroom at one thirty. It was a windy day and doors were banging and dustbin lids flying. And there stood this student with Sir and the Headmaster, who were both wreathed in smiles like the cats on the roof tops. And we were

25   quiet. We sat down in our seats without the dicky bird of a sound, not because the Head was there, but because of her.

    I don't much notice how people look. I either like them or I don't. Danny and Crumble and Pitthead have

30   a nice look. Martin Kneeshaw, Linda Stoatway and Lorraine Fairchild have a horrid look. Some people say that our Beryl is pretty. I wouldn't know. But looking at this one was like looking at sunshine or a shop full of sweets when you're starving. The Head nodded to us

35   and went away smiling and humming to himself.

    What happened to the other one?

    'Miss Prebble was unable to come to this school after all, so I want you to welcome Miss Honeywell, instead.'

    'Good afternoon, Miss Honeywell.'

40   'It's absolutely splendid to meet you all. Please call me Jenny.'

    Aaaaaaaahhhhhhh murmured round the room. Pitthead was saying, 'Jenny, Jenny', in a pleased way and Danny was gazing at her as if he'd seen a miracle.

45   Sir was grinning from ear to ear and that's a pretty fair distance for a grin. She had one of those upper-class voices, the sort that makes Dad drop all his aitches and be dead common, but it sounded all right on her. Anything would sound all right on her. Sir said:

Reading extract continued

50 'Actually, I think they'll call you Miss. They usually
do. Now, I expect you'd like to meet them. Continue
with some work in your folders, children,while Miss
Honeywell – er – Jenny comes round to talk to you ...'
'Me, Miss.'
65 'No, me, first.'
'Me. Me. Me.'

Questions

In the first part of the story (lines 1–19), the class is told about the student's visit.

1 Choose the best ending for each of these sentences.

a) The student was coming to the class:

> A for one afternoon
> B for the next five weeks
> C for the rest of the term

b) Tyke did not like this student teacher because:
> A she did not look very friendly
> B she was ugly
> C she looked down on the children

c) The children did not like student teachers taking the class because:
> A they did not know how to teach
> B they found it hard to control the pupils
> C they had a lot to learn

(3 marks)

2 Which of Pitthead's **actions** showed that he did not like the idea of the student coming to the class?   *(1 mark)*

3 a) Explain how you think Tyke felt about 'Sir', the class teacher.   *(1 mark)*

b) Write down an expression that backs up your answer.   *(1 mark)*

4 During this conversation, the class teacher becomes angry with the class. Find the simile which shows this.

(1 mark)

5 How did the class react to the teacher's anger? **Answer in your own words.**   *(1 mark)*

6 This part of the story is made up of a conversation between the teacher and the class. Write down **ONE** difference between the way the teacher talks and the way the pupils talk.   *(1 mark)*

In the second part of the story (lines 20–66), another student arrives and the class reacts very differently to her.

7 In your own words, describe the way in which the class came into the room after lunchtime. *(2 marks)*

8 What was the weather like outside? *(1 mark)*

9 a) **In your own words,** explain Tyke's feelings on seeing Miss Honeywell for the first time. *(1 mark)*

    b) Find a simile from the passage that backs up your answer. *(1 mark)*

10 Write down the words which show that the Headmaster was pleased with the new student. *(1 mark)*

11 At the end of the passage, how does the writer help us to understand that the children were very keen to talk to Miss Honeywell? *(1 mark)*

12 Decide whether each of these sentences is **true** or **false** or whether you **can't tell** from the passage. Copy this table into your exercise book and complete it.

	true	false	can't tell
a) The class was very quiet because the Headmaster had come into the room.			
b) Tyke Tiler always judged people by their appearance.			
c) Both the class teacher and the Headmaster had cats.			
d) When Miss Honeywell came into the classroom the children were doing work in their folders.			
e) The class liked the sound of Miss Honeywell's voice.			
f) Miss Honeywell was a very good teacher.			

(6 marks)

13 Complete this summary of the second part of the story by putting **one or more words** in each gap. You may use words from the story or your own words. Write your answers in a list, using the numbers given in each gap.

The noisy pupils became ____1____ when Miss Honeywell, the student teacher, entered the classroom, because they had been expecting ____2____ instead. All the children were ____3____ when they saw her. She showed a very ____4____ manner towards them and invited them to call her ____5____ . One of the pupils who took an instant liking to her was called ____6____ . During this time their teacher kept ____7____ . While the class worked on their folders Miss Honeywell came round to ____8____ to them.

(8 marks)

Total – 30 marks

Taking a closer look

Standard English and dialect

Question six asked about the differences between the way the teacher and the pupils spoke.

You will have noticed that people speak differently in different parts of the country. The name for this kind of language is **dialect**. On the other hand, Standard English is the form of English that is used and understood everywhere.

For example, Tyke says:

> **'Why we gotter 'ave students?'**

In Standard English, this would be: 'Why do we have to have students?'

Some writers have written whole stories and poems in the dialect of a particular town or area. One you might enjoy reading is called 'Colour Prejudice' by Doris Watt which is set in Dundee and tells of a woman who meets a Martian. Here's how it begins:

> *If ye'd asked Muggie Robertson if she believed in wee green men fae Mars, she wud hav telt y tae awa and no be daft, because Muggie kent fur a fact they were mair like purple, and how she came tae ken wis like this.*
>
> *She wus aye in the habit o takkin her doag fur a run in the Baxter Park afore she went tae hur bed, and that's whut she wis daein o the Seeterday nicht she met the spacemen. (This was back in the days, mind, when a wummin could tak a turn around the park without getting set on by a gang o neds.)*

For practice

1   Rewrite the passage in Standard English.

2   Which version do your prefer? Why?

Follow on

Topic for discussion

In groups, make a list of dialect words or expressions used in your area. Pick out your favourite words and explain why you like them.

Writing

1   Try writing a story using some dialect from your own area or from another area you know well.

OR

2   Write the script of a conversation between two speakers, one speaking in Standard English and the other in dialect. You might then read out your script to the rest of your group or to the whole class.

Chapter 6

The Indian in the Cupboard

The main character in this story by Lynne Reid Banks is a boy called Omri. When the story begins, it is Omri's birthday, and he gets presents from his family and from his best friend, Patrick.

Reading extract

1   It was, without a
doubt, *very* kind
of Patrick to give
Omri anything
5   at all, let alone a
second-hand
plastic Red
Indian which he
himself had
10   finished with.
But when Patrick
brought his
present to school on Omri's birthday, Omri was
disappointed. He tried not to show it, but he was. He
15   put the Indian in his pocket and forgot about it.

After school there was a family tea, and all the
excitement of his presents from his parents and his two
older brothers. He was given his dearest wish – a
skateboard complete with kick-board and cryptonic

20 wheels from his mum and dad, and from his eldest
brother, Adiel, a helmet. Gillon, his other brother,
hadn't bought him anything because he had no money.
So when Gillon's turn came to give Omri a present,
Omri was very surprised when a large parcel was put
25 before him.
   'What is it?'
   'Have a look. I found it in the alley.'
   The alley was a narrow pasage that ran along the
bottom of the garden where the dustbins stood. The
30 three boys used to play there sometimes, and
occasionally found treasures that other – perhaps richer
– neighbours had thrown away.
   Inside was a small white metal cupboard with a
mirror in the door, the kind you see over the basin in
35 old-fashioned bathrooms.
   You might suppose Omri would once again be
disappointed, because the cupboard was fairly plain,
and, except for a shelf, completely empty, but oddly
enough he was very pleased with it. He loved cupboards
40 of any sort because of the fun of keeping things in them.
   The night, Omri put the cupboard on his bedside
table, and opening it, looked inside thoughtfuly. What
would he put in it?
   'Why don't you pop this in?' his mother suggested,
45 and opened her hand. In it was Patrick's Red Indian. 'I
found it when I was putting your trousers in the
washing machine.'
   Omri carefully stood the Indian on the shelf. Then
he locked the cupboard door. He turned the light out

50 and lay down on his side, looking at the cupboard. He felt very content. Just as he was dropping off to sleep his eyes snapped open. He had thought he heard a little noise ... but no. All was quiet. His eyes closed again.

In the morning there was no doubt about it. The
55 noise actually woke him.

He lay perfectly still in the dawn light staring at the cupboard, from which was now coming a most extraordinary series of sounds. A pattering; a tapping; a scrabbling; and – surely – a high-pitched noise like –
60 well, almost like a tiny voice?

He lay still for a long time, wondering. Had he imagined it? The noise did not start again. At last he cautiously turned the key and opened the cupboard door.

The Indian was gone.
65 Omri sat up sharply in bed and peered into the dark corners. Suddenly he saw him. But he wasn't on the shelf any more, he was in the bottom of the
70 cupboard. And he wasn't standing upright. He was crouching in the
75 darkest corner, half hidden by the front of the cupboard. And he was alive.

Questions

In the first paragraph of the passage, we are told how Omri gets the 'Indian' mentioned in the title of the book. Choose A, B or C for your answers.

1 In line 2, the word 'very' is in italics when we are told about Patrick's gift.

How does this make the writer sound?
A excited
B sarcastic
C impressed   *(1 mark)*

2 Patrick was not really being 'very kind' when he gave Omri the plastic Red Indian because:
A Patrick had plenty of money to buy a better present
B Patrick was just getting rid of an old toy he did not want
C Patrick knew Omri did not like plastic figures
                                                          (1 mark)

In the second part of the passage we are told how Omri gets the 'cupboard' mentioned in the title of the book.

3 Write down the phrase from paragraph 2 which tells you Omri had been hoping to get the skateboard.   *(1 mark)*

4 Do you think Omri's brother Adiel knew what present his parents were giving Omri? Give a reason for your answer.   *(1 mark)*

5 Do you think Omri was expecting a present from his brother Gillon? Give a reason for your answer.   *(1 mark)*

6 Which of the following is closest in meaning to the word 'treasures' as it is used in line 31?

   A Valuable objects which people had thrown away by mistake

   B Things which had been thrown away but were interesting to the boys

   C Things which the boys found which they could sell for money   *(1 mark)*

7 Decide whether each sentence is **true** or **false** or whether you **can't tell** from the passage. Copy this table into your exercise book and complete it.

	true	false	can't tell
a) Omri was disappointed when he first saw the cupboard.		✓	
b) Omri had never had a cupboard of his own before.			✓
c) Omri was looking forward to keeping things in the little cupboard.	✓		
d) Omri's mother had found the plastic Red Indian in the dustbin.		✓	

                                           (4 marks)

The third section of the passage tells of what happens when Omri takes the Red Indian and the cupboard to his bedroom.

8 Write down the sentence from paragraph 9 (lines 48–53) that tells us Omri had had an enjoyable birthday. *(1 mark)*

9 In line 53, the writer uses three dots (called an ellipsis). Pick out the answer you think comes closest to describing the effect of this:

   A The dots show a word or words has been left out

   B The dots speed up the pace of the sentence

   C The dots suggest a pause as if Omri is listening for a
     few seconds   *(1 mark)*

10 Do you think the noise from the cupboard was **louder**
    or **softer** in the morning? Give a reason for your answer.
                                               (1 mark)

11 Certain words, such as 'buzz', *sound* like their meanings.
    From paragraph 12 (lines 56–60), pick out **ONE** word
    which sounds like its meaning.   *(1 mark)*

12 'The Indian was gone'. (line 64)
    Explain **ONE** way in which the writer has made this
    sentence stand out.   *(1 mark)*

13 Omri moves and thinks very **quickly** when he finds the
    Indian has disappeared from the shelf.
    From the last paragraph, pick out **TWO adverbs** which
    suggest this idea of speed.   *(2 marks)*

14 Here is a summary of the passage. Suggest **one word or
    two words** to fill each space. You may use your own
    words or words from the passage. Write your answers in
    a list using the numbers given in each space.

Omri felt _____1_____ when his friend Patrick gave him a
second-hand plastic Red Indian for his _____2_____ . However,
he felt better when he went home and got a _____3_____ from
his parents and a _____4_____ from his _____5_____ brother. He
was _____6_____ to get a large parcel from his other brother,
Gillon, since he had had no money. The parcel contained a
small cupboard which Gillon had found in the _____7_____
where the dustbins were kept. Although the cupboard was
quite _____8_____ and contained only a shelf, Omri felt
_____9_____ because he could keep things in it. When he went
to bed, he put it on his _____10_____ table and placed the plastic
Red Indian on the shelf. Then he _____11_____ the cupboard. In
the morning there were strange _____12_____ coming from the

cupboard, and when Omri opened the door, he ___13___ the Indian had come to life.

(13 marks)

Total – 30 marks

Taking a closer look

Characters

'**Character**' is the name given to a person in a story. One of the main things that makes us enjoy a story is the people, or 'characters' the writer creates. Sometimes, you may feel you know more about characters in a story than about some real people that you know!

A good writer makes us care about the characters in the story and the reader becomes interested in what happens to them. The writer can also show what a character is like by filling in a few important details.

For example, in the extract we are told that Omri's eldest brother, Adiel, gives Omri a skateboard helmet for his birthday. This tells us something about Adiel as a character.

You could write it like this:

Adiel is a thoughtful character.

We know this because he gives Omri a helmet to go with his skateboard which his parents are giving Omri. The helmet will let Omri use his skateboard safely.

Now write about the other characters listed below in the same way. First, choose the word which you think describes the character best, and then write down a reason using information from the passage.

> **Hint**
> Sometimes there may be more than one possible answer. Remember to think carefully about the reason for the answer you choose.

Use a **dictionary** to check what the words mean if you do not know them.

1 **Patrick** is a **kind / mean / selfish** character

We know this because . . .

2 **Omri** is a **good-natured / imaginative / sulky** character

We know this because . . .

3 **Gillon** is a **resourceful** / **thoughtless** / **stupid** character

We know this because . . .

4 **Omri's mother** is a **strict** / **kind** / **thoughful** character.

We know this because . . .

Follow on

Topics for discussion

1 Write down three reasons why you would like to read more of this story.

Discuss your reasons with your class or group.

2 Think of an object which is more interesting than it looks. Tell your group or class about it.

Writing

1 Write a story of your own about a toy that comes to life.

2 'The best present ever'.

Write about either:

a) Something which you yourself were very pleased to get

OR

b) Something which you gave to someone else which you know made the person happy.

Explain what the thing was and why it was such a success.

Chapter 7

Double Act

'Double Act' by Jacqueline Wilson is the story of ten-year old twin girls, Ruby and Garnet, whose mother has died. Their names have a similar meaning: both ruby and garnet are red gem stones. However, although the twins look identical, they have very different personalities, as you will discover in this extract. The twins tell the story in turn, with Garnet's words printed in *italics* to show where she takes over from Ruby.

Reading extract

1   We're twins. I'm Ruby. She's Garnet.

We're identical. There's very few people who can tell us apart. Well, until we start talking. I tend to go on and on. Garnet is much quieter.

5   *That's because I can't get a word in edgeways.*

We're going to be famous someday, you bet. So I've started writing our life-story already. It's funny, Garnet is usually the one who writes stuff. Her writing's neater than mine. So often I get her to do my schoolwork. She

10   doesn't mind.

Yes, I do.

I was rifling through one of the boxes of books upstairs and right at the bottom there was this lovely fat red book, ruby red, with a leather spine and one

15   word picked out in gold lettering: ACCOUNTS.

Reading extract continued

I though it was the title but when I opened it up there were just all these blank pages.

I asked Dad what had happened to the story and he said it wasn't a proper book at all. Accounts are sums.
20 You add up everything you've bought. That's keeping accounts.

'Only I don't like keeping accounts. I just feel guilty seeing how much I've spent,' said Dad. 'You can have it to scribble in, twins.'

25 So I'm scribbling away.

I'm not.

Yes, you are. I keep letting you have a turn. And I'm not just writing about me, I'm writing about us. Giving an account of ourselves. Hey Garnet, find a dictionary
30 and look up the word 'account'.

Account: 1. A verbal or written report, description, or narration of some occurrence, event, etcetera.

Yeah! That's exactly what I'm doing. Writing an account of our lives.

35   Everything's a bit boring right this minute but maybe soon we'll somehow get our big chance and we'll achieve our lifetime's ambition and be actresses.

    I don't want to be an actress.

    Of course we want to be actresses. Honestly, Garnet,
40 give over jogging me. (She can be a bit stupid and shy at times. She doesn't think we'll ever make it as flashy film stars, but I keep telling her all we need is CONFIDENCE. She keeps going on at me now, saying she doesn't want to be a star. Well that's mad. She can't mean it. Who on earth
45 wouldn't want to show off all day in front of the camera and go to posh parties every night with all the other stars?)

    We'll live in our own flash flat with masses of flowers in every room and huge boxes of chocs to dip into whenever we fancy, and we'll wear ruby-red sequin
50 frocks and ruby jewellery to match – OK OK Garnet, you can have garnets, only they're not as precious and valuable and sparkly, are they?

    That's not what you wanted to say? Well, what do you want to say then? All right. You write your bit now.
55 Go on. Here you are. Get cracking. You write about you.

    I don't know what to put.

    I'm not used to writing about me. It's always us.

    I do like writing, though. I like making up plays and I don't mind acting them out when it's just Ruby and me and
60 *we're totally private and imagining it so it could almost be actually happening, but I can't bear proper acting.*

    Ruby and I were twin sheep in the nativity play when we were still in the Infants and it was one of the most truly awful experiences of my life.

> **Reading extract continued**

65 *Not the most awful of course.*
That was when
Look, you're not writing any of
that sad stuff. I won't let you. This
is me again. Ruby. It's my turn
70 now. You have to be able to take
turns fairly when you're twins.

Questions

Section A

In the first part of the passage (lines 1–11), Ruby introduces herself and her sister, Garnet.

1 Complete these sentences by choosing the best ending.

  a) Garnet does not talk as much as Ruby because:
    A She can't think of as much to say as Ruby can
    B Ruby talks so much Garnet doesn't get the chance to talk
    C Garnet likes to listen to Ruby

  b) Ruby began writing the twins' life story because:
    A she thought that writing a book might make her famous
    B she was afraid they might forget the things they had done
    C she was sure they would be famous one day

(2 marks)

2 Decide whether each of these sentences is **true** or **false**. Copy this table into your exercise book and complete it.

	true	false
a) Ruby knows Garnet is better at writing than she is.	✓	
b) Garnet does not mind doing Ruby's homework for her.		✓

(2 marks)

In the second part of the story (lines 12–34), Ruby describes finding the 'Accounts' book.

3 Find words in this section of the story which have the following meanings:

  a) searching

  b) the back of a book. *(2 marks)*

4 What does the phrase 'picked out' in line 15 mean? Choose A, B or C for your answer.
  A selected
  B marked out in a colour
  C removed *(1 mark)*

5 Explain **ONE** reason why Ruby thinks the Accounts books is 'lovely.' *(1 mark)*

6 Choose the best ending for this sentence:

  The accounts book had blank pages because . . .
  A it had been put away upstairs and forgotten
  B Ruby's Dad didn't like seeing how much money he had spent
  C it was too good to write in *(1 mark)*

In the third part of the story (lines 35–71), Ruby and Garnet talk about acting and being actresses.

7 Explain **ONE** reason why Ruby thinks it would be wonderful to be a film star. (1 mark)

8 Look at these sentences about this section of the passage. Decide whether each sentence is **true** or **false** or whether you **can't tell** from the passage. Copy this table into your exercise book and complete it.

	true	false	can't tell
a) Ruby wants to be an actress more than Garnet does.	✓		
b) Ruby believes everyone enjoys showing off as much as she does.	✓		
c) Garnet enjoys writing plays.	✓	✓	
d) Garnet also enjoyed being in the infants' nativity play.			✓
e) Ruby is very talented at acting and drama.			✓
f) Garnet finds it hard to write as herself, rather than as a twin.	✓		

Partys

(6 marks)

Section B

Here is a summary of the passage. Suggest **one word or two words** to fill each space. You may use your own words or words from the passage. Write your answers in a list using the numbers in each space.

People can only tell the twins apart since Ruby ____1____ more than Garnet. Ruby believes they will be ____2____ one day, and so she has started writing their ____3____ . She would like to be an ____4____ . Ruby thinks it would be fun to show off in front of the ____5____ and go to ____6____ .

She thinks she and Garnet could live in a beautiful flat where they would eat ____7____ and they would ____8____ sparkling red dresses and jewellery. However, Garnet says she would not like to be an actress, but she prefers ____9____ plays. She even found acting in the infants' nativity play a ____10____ experience.

(10 marks)

Section C

The author shows the difference between the two girls' personalities both in *what they say* and *how they say it*. You can use either of these as examples for your evidence in the following question.

1 a) Write down a word from the following list which you think describes Ruby's personality:

> selfish   bossy   thoughtful
> outgoing   mean   lively

b) Give an example from the story as evidence for your answer.   *(2 marks)*

2 a) Write down a word from the following list which you think describes Garnet's personality.

> unhappy   shy   creative
> quarrelsome   irritable   thoughtful

b) Give an example from the story as evidence for your answer.   *(2 marks)*

Total – 30 marks

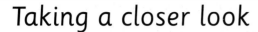

Taking a closer look

Abbreviations

In direct speech, some words are run together to show how we actually say them. For example, 'I'm' (line 1) shows the way the words 'I am' are spoken. An **apostrophe** is used where the 'a' of 'am' is missed out.

In this story, the writer aims to give the impression that the characters are *talking* to us. She uses quite a number of abbreviations.

For practice (1)

In each example, write out the full words which have been abbreviated.

You should always check the sentence which the abbreviation comes from, as sometimes the same abbreviation comes from a different pair of words.

   1 we're (line 1)

   2 she's (line 1)

   3 that's (line 5)

   4 can't (line 5)

   5 I've (line 6)

   6 it's (line 7)

   7 doesn't (line 10)

   8 we'll (line 36)

9 don't (line 38)

10 won't (68)

For practice (2)

Rewrite the following sentences, including at least one abbreviation. Remember to put an apostrophe into each abbreviation. Underline your abbreviations.

1 Garnet did not want to become an actress.

2 He is nicer than his brother.

3 Ruby would not let Garnet speak.

4 I have got a twin brother.

5 He can not find his bag.

6 They are going to write their life story.

7 I would like to become a footballer.

8 I do not think that you are telling the truth.

Follow on

Topics for discussion

1 Write down three reasons why you would like to read more of this story. Discuss your reasons with your class or group.

2 Discuss in your groups the advantages and disadvantages of being an identical twin. (If there are twins in your class, you could interview them.)

Writing

1 Write a story in which identical twins are mixed up.

OR

2 If you have siblings (brothers and / or sisters), write about your relationships with them. If you are an only child, write about the advantages and disadvantages of this.

Chapter 8

Buddy

'Buddy' by Nigel Hinton is an exciting and moving story about a fourteen-year old boy called Buddy who gets caught up without meaning to in his father's life of crime. This is the opening chapter.

Reading extract

1   Buddy stole the money from his mother's purse just before he left for school. His mother was in the kitchen clearing up the breakfast things and his father was still in bed.

5   He tiptoed into the front room and slipped the purse out of her handbag. He clicked it open and took out a £5 note. A wave of disgust swept through him. Only two weeks ago he'd vowed to himself that he was going to stop shop-lifting and here he was stealing from his

10 own mother. He hadn't done that since he was a little kid and had sometimes nicked the odd ten pence. He

15 was turning into a real thief. There must be something the

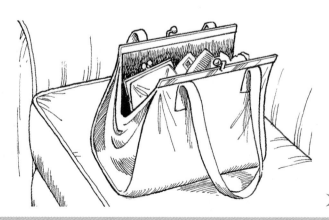

matter with him. First, the shop-lifting. He'd done it a
20 couple of times with some other boys from school.
They had stopped but he'd gone on doing it alone. And
now, this.

He heard his mum come out of the kitchen and, in a
moment of panic, he fumbled with the catch on the
25 purse. It would't close properly so he just chucked it back
in the bag still open. He put the handbag back on the
sofa, crumpled the note in his pocket, and went out of
the room. His mum was in the hall putting on her coat.

'Hurry up, you're late,' she said and then called up
30 the stairs. 'Terry!'

There was no answer from his dad. His mum called
out again and then started up the stairs.

Buddy put on his shoes and while he was tying up
the laces he heard angry voices coming from upstairs.
35 Another row. Recently, there'd been more rows than
anything else. He hated to hear his mum and dad
shouting like that.

'I'm going,' he called. There was no reply so he went
out of the front door, slamming it behind him.

40 The morning at school was terrible. The money for
the class trip didn't have to be handed in until
lunchtime so he knew he could still change his mind.
He went through the arguments again and again. He
could take the money back. His mum was bound to
45 have noticed it had gone – money was precious since
the factory had closed and his dad had lost his job. He
could always leave it lying on the floor, as if it had
fallen out of her bag.

Reading extract continued

He didn't even want to go on the trip – £4 to see
50 some stupid castle and safari park. On the other hand,
he didn't want to stay behind again. It would be the
third thing he'd missed this term alone. The other
times – the visit to the theatre and the trip to the Three
Counties Agricultural Show – he'd been the only one
55 not going from 3E. He'd had to join another class for
the day and it had been awful.

This time he hadn't even bothered to ask for the
money. He knew what his parents would say 'We can't
afford it.' Well, it was all right for them. They still had
60 the things they wanted. They both smoked; that cost a
fortune nowadays, and it was bad for them. And his
dad had started going out to the pub in the evenings.
His mum moaned about that, saying it was a waste of
money and he was mixing with the wrong crowd again,
65 but it didn't stop him doing it.

> ### Reading extract continued
>
> The more Buddy thought about it, the more it seemed that he had right on his side. If his mum and dad had to give up smoking and drinking for a couple of days – so much the better. It would be good for
> 70 them.
>
> Still, he hesitated a moment when Mr Normington said, 'Right, 3E, hands up the people who brought the money for the trip to Newton Castle.' Buddy looked round and saw everybody's hand go up. Then he raised
> 75 his, too.

Questions

The first part of the passage (lines 1–39) takes place at Buddy's house in the morning.

1 Complete these sentences by choosing the best ending.

a) Buddy had an opportunity to steal the money from his mother's handbag because:
   A   his mother was still in bed
   B   his parents were arguing upstairs
   C   his mother was in the kitchen clearing up

b) Buddy felt he was becoming 'a real thief' because:
   A   he sometimes went shop-lifting with boys at school
   B   he had continued shop-lifting alone
   C   he had always stolen small sums from his mother

   c) When Buddy's father stayed in bed, Buddy's mother:
      A slammed the front door and left
      B told Buddy to go and speak to him
      C went upstairs and shouted at him   *(3 marks)*

2 a) Write down a word from the second paragraph (lines 5–22) which shows Buddy tried to be very quiet when he went into the front room.   *(1 mark)*

    b) Write down a single word from the second paragraph which shows how Buddy felt about stealing the money.   *(1 mark)*

3 **In your own words,** explain **ONE** piece of evidence to show Buddy had stolen things before.   *(1 mark)*

4 Write down a word from the third paragraph (lines 23–28) which shows how Buddy feels when his mother nearly catches him with her purse.   *(1 mark)*

5 From paragraph three, find a word that means:

    a) handled in a clumsy way

    b) threw quickly and carelessly.   *(2 marks)*

6 a) Did Buddy close the door loudly or quietly? *(1 mark)*

    b) Write down the word which tells you the answer to question 6 a).   *(1 mark)*

    c) Suggest **ONE** reason why Buddy closed the door in this way.   *(1 mark)*

The second part of the passage (lines 40–75) takes place at Buddy's school.

7 Look at these sentences about lines 40–56. Decide whether each sentence is **true** or **false** or whether you **can't tell** from the passage. Copy this table into your exercise book and complete it.

	true	false	can't tell
a) Buddy had the whole morning to decide whether to return the money.	✓		
b) Buddy thought his mother was unlikely to notice the money was missing.		✓	
c) Buddy was very keen to see Newton Castle.		✓	
d) Buddy had missed out on school trips before.	✓		
e) There were other children at the school who were as poor as Buddy.		✓	

(5 marks)

8 a) Read lines 57–65. What reason did Buddy think his parents would give for refusing him the money?

(1 mark)

b) **In your own words**, explain why Buddy did not accept the reason. *(2 marks)*

9 Explain **in your own words** why Buddy thought 'he had right on his side' (line 67) when he stole the money.

(2 marks)

10 Read the last paragraph.

Explain how the writer makes it clear that Buddy 'hesitated' about putting his name down for the trip.

(2 marks)

11 Here is a summary of the whole passage. Suggest **one word or two words** to fill each space. You may use your own words or words from the passage. Write your answers in a list using the numbers in each space.

Buddy stole money from his mother's purse as he wanted to go on a ____1____. His mother nearly caught him when she came out of the ____2____ and Buddy had no time to ____3____ the purse. Buddy knew that money was short in his family as his father had lost his job at the ____4____. Buddy thought of returning the £5 note by leaving it on the ____5____. However, when his teacher asked who had brought their money, Buddy ____6____ his hand along with the others.

(6 marks)

Total – 30 marks

Taking a closer look

Using your own words

For practice (1)

For each of the following words from the passage suggest another similar word or phrase which could be used instead without changing the meaning:

- ★ stole (line 1)
- ★ vowed (line 8)
- ★ row (line 35)
- ★ precious (line 45)
- ★ awful (line 56)
- ★ moaned (line 63)

For practice (2)

Write out the following sentences, using **one word** or **more than one word** of your own instead of the underlined words.

a) Buddy <u>tiptoed</u> into the front room and <u>slipped</u> the purse out of her handbag.

b) He <u>put</u> the handbag back on the <u>sofa</u> and <u>crumpled</u> the note into his pocket.

c) His <u>mum</u> was <u>bound</u> to have <u>noticed</u> it had <u>gone</u>.

For practice (3) More Difficult!

The following extracts are taken from the passage. Pupils in a class were asked to explain each extract using their own words. Write down the letter of the answer you think is best:

1 'There must be something the matter with him.' (lines 17–19)

   a) Buddy thought he might be coming down with an illness.

   b) Buddy didn't feel guilty as he couldn't help stealing.

   c) Buddy knew his stealing was becoming a real problem.

2 'He went through the arguments again and again.' (line 43)

   a) He kept remembering the rows his parents had.

   b) He kept thinking of the reasons why he should put the money back.

c) He was upset because he couldn't decide what to do.

3 'This time he hadn't even bothered to ask for the money.' (line 57)

    a) Buddy couldn't be bothered arguing with his parents about money.

    b) Buddy knew there was no point in asking for money.

    c) Buddy felt ashamed to ask his parents for more money.

Follow on

Topics for discussion

1 Write down **THREE** reasons why you would like to read more of this story.

Discuss your reasons with your class or group.

2 Right or Wrong? Look at all the evidence in the story, and discuss how far Buddy was right or wrong to steal money for the school trip.

Writing

1 Write your own account of what happened when Buddy went home from school that night.

2 'Honesty is the Best Policy'. Write a story with this theme.

Chapter 9

Meet the Polar Bear

As this passage explains, polar bears have a remarkable ability to survive in harsh icy conditions.

Reading extract

1 The polar bear is the largest **carnivore** living on land. It
lives in the freezing cold climate of the Arctic, close to
the sea or on the sea ice. Its thick white coat acts as
camouflage in the snow, as well as keeping it warm.

5 Polar bears live all round the Arctic, wherever there
is ice on the sea. Although they spend most of their
time on the ice, they are excellent swimmers. They can
swim for hundreds of kilometres from one ice floe to
the next. Their waterproof coat and thick layer of fat

10 enable them to float easily. They can also dive
underwater for as long as two minutes.

Polar bears mate in April or June, and the females are
pregnant for six and a half to nine months. In
November, a pregnant female polar bear digs a den,

15 usually in a snow drift. At the end of a passage two to
six metres long, she makes a chamber where she will
stay until spring comes. Some females use the same den
year after year.

Although female polar bears stay in their dens for four

20 or five months, they do not really hibernate. Their heart
slows from seventy to about eight beats per minute, but

> Note
Carnivore: *a meat-eating animal*

73

their temperature and breathing stay near normal. Animals that do hibernate can take several days to wake up, but a dozing polar bear can wake in an instant.

25   The cubs are born about six weeks after the female enters her den. There are usually two cubs. Sometimes there is only one, and very rarely three or even four. The newborn cubs are tiny – about the size of rats – and they weigh 600–700 grams. They are blind and deaf,

30 and completely helpless. Polar bear cubs open their eyes when they are about thirty-three days old. They start to hear after twenty-six days.

    Although it is warmer in the den than outside, the temperature still falls below freezing. The mother keeps

35 her cubs warm by cuddling them in her arms and by breathing on them. She feeds them with her milk, which is very high in fat. The mother does not feed at all. She lives off the fat she has stored in her body during the summer.

Questions

1 Decide whether each of these sentences is **true** or **false** or whether you **can't tell** from the passage. Copy this table into your exercise book and complete it.

	true	false	can't tell
a) The polar bear is a meat-eating animal.			
b) Polar bears like to live near ice.			
c) Pregnant polar bears spend the winter in a chamber dug into the snow.			
d) Polar bears go into a deep sleep during hibernation.			
e) No polar bear has ever given birth to more than four cubs at one time.			

(5 marks)

2 Write down **TWO** ways in which the polar bear's thick white coat is helpful to it. *(2 marks)*

3 Polar bears are 'excellent swimmers' (line 7). Write down **TWO** pieces of evidence for this. *(2 marks)*

4 **In your own words**, give one reason why polar bears are able to swim so well. *(1 mark)*

5 The writer says that female polar bears 'do not really hibernate' (line 20). **In your own words**, explain **ONE** difference between these bears and animals that do hibernate. *(1 mark)*

6 How does the writer help us to understand how small the polar bear cubs are when they have just been born? *(1 mark)*

7 Write down **TWO** ways in which the mother keeps her cubs warm. *(2 marks)*

8 Why has the mother no need to feed during the time she is with her cubs in the den under the snow? *(1 mark)*

9 Here is a summary of some of the information in the passage. Fill in the gaps, using one word in each space. You may use your own words or the words of the passage. Write your answers in a list using the numbers in each space.

The polar bear is the largest animal that lives on land and eats ____1____. A female is pregnant for at least ____2____ months. During November a pregnant female will make a ____3____ under the snow. About ____4____ weeks later, she will usually give birth to ____5____ tiny cubs. When the cubs are born they are both ____6____ and ____7____.

(7 marks)

10 From anywhere in the passage, find a word which fits each of the following meanings:

a) weather conditions

b) a large area of frozen sea water

c) sleeping lightly *(3 marks)*

Total– 25 marks

Taking a closer look

Paragraphs (1)

The passage on Polar Bears is divided into six paragraphs. A paragraph is a collection of sentences which are all about

76

one subject. When a writer wants to move onto a new point, he or she begins a new paragraph. If a piece of writing was written without paragraphs, it would be very difficult to read!

There are two ways of making it clear that you are beginning a new paragraph:

★ In handwriting, take a new line and **indent** – that is, start a few centimetres in from the margin.
★ When using a computer, many people do not indent the first line, but leave a bigger gap (known as 'double spacing') between paragraphs.

Writing by hand   *Using the computer*

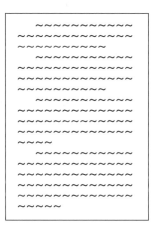 

For practice

a) Try to sum up in a few words what each paragraph in the Polar Bears passage deals with. Copy this table into your exercise book and complete it. Two have been done for you already.

Paragraph	What is it about
1	The kind of area that polar bears live in
2	
3	
4	
5	
6	How the mother looks after her cubs

b) The passage that follows describes the life cycle of the polar bear, but it has not been divided into paragraphs. Rewrite it in **THREE** paragraphs.

* The first paragraph should describe how helpless the cubs are.
* The second should deal with the subject of food.
* The last paragraph should talk about how the bears develop as they grow up.

The Life Cycle of a Polar Bear

At first the polar bear cubs are very helpless. They are dependent on their mother to feed them with milk and they cannot hear or see. It takes more than a month for their eyes to open. After winter the search for food becomes the mother's main task. By March the fat on her body has been used up and she is much thinner. The mother will make for the sea where she will hunt for seals. At that stage the cubs will wait in the snow for their mother to come back and feed them. As they grow older the cubs become more independent. During their second year they will start to hunt and soon they will leave their mother to spend time on their own. After five years, the females will be old enough to have their first cubs and the life cycle of the polar bear will begin all over again.

Follow on

Topic for discussion

Polar bears like to roam over large distances and so they often do not adapt well to living in zoos. However, if they are not kept in zoos, most people will never see one. Discuss whether animals like polar bears should or should not be kept in zoos.

Follow on continued

Writing

1 Use the Internet or an encyclopedia to find out about the life cycle of another animal that you like. Write a short account similar to the one on the polar bear.

2 Imagine you are a photographer who has been sent to the Arctic to photograph polar bears for a wildlife magazine. Describe what happens.

Chapter 10

Football, the Global Game

This passage talks about the worldwide popularity of football and traces the career of the famous Brazilian player Ronaldo.

Reading extract

1 Soccer is the most popular sport on Earth. It is played by millions of people around the world

5 – on green fields, tropical beaches and dusty roads. It is played by the rich and the poor, the young and the old, by men and

10 women of every colour, religion and background. Football brings people together. You can go anywhere in the world –

15 places where people speak a different language, eat different food or belong to a different religion – but say the word 'Beckham' and they will smile and understand. Soccer has a culture all of its own.

On 22 September 1976, a boy named Ronaldo De

20 Lima was born in a poor neighbourhood in Rio, Brazil.

Reading extract continued

Ronnie – as he was to become known – was brought up
by his mother, a waitress at a pizza restaurant. Almost
as soon as he could walk the young Ronnie spent most
of his time playing football on the streets with his
25 friends. As he got older, this worried Ronnie's mother,
who wanted her son to spend more time studying. But
it soon became clear Ronnie had a special talent. When
he was thirteen he told his friends: 'One day I will
become the best in the world.' At sixteen he scored his
30 first goal for Brazil. Today many would agree he has
fulfilled his ambition.

The famous former Liverpool football manager Bill
Shankly once said: 'Some people believe football is a
matter of life and death . . . I can assure you it's much,
35 much more important than that.'

The soccer World Cup in Japan and Korea in 2002
was watched on TV by nearly 30 billion people around
the globe. More people watched the eight-week
tournament than watched any other event in history. It
40 was broadcast in 213 countries with each live match
averaging a TV audience of around 356 million people.
By the time Ronaldo scored to sink Germany in the
World Cup final, more than a billion homes had
switched on to watch.

Questions

1 'Football is the most popular sport on Earth.' (lines 1–2). Write down **ONE** piece of evidence from the first paragraph that backs up this comment. *(1 mark)*

2 In the first paragraph the writer mentions several pairs of opposites.

Write down **TWO** of these. Lay out your answer like this:

a) _____ and _____

b) _____ and _____ *(2 marks)*

3 a) 'Football brings people together' (lines 12–13). **In your own words**, explain what you think this means. *(2 marks)*

   b) What example is given in paragraph one to prove this point? *(1 mark)*

4 a) 'Soccer has a culture all of its own.' (line 18). Choose from A, B and C to decide what this sentence means.
   A there are clear rules about how the game should be played
   B people from different backgrounds and countries share an interest in football
   C football is very different from other sports. *(1 mark)*

5 Write down **THREE** facts about Ronaldo's background from paragraph two (lines 19–31). *(3 marks)*

6 What was the earliest sign that Ronaldo might become a footballer? *(1 mark)*

7 a) Write down the word which shows how Ronaldo's mother felt about his interest in football while he was still a schoolboy. *(1 mark)*

b) **In your own words,** explain why she felt this way.

(1 mark)

8 Copy out the sentence that shows Ronaldo had a very clear idea of what he was aiming at in life. *(1 mark)*

9 a) What is unusual about Bill Shankly's comment in lines 33–35? *(1 mark)*

b) Explain the connection between this point and the paragraph that follows on from it (lines 36–44).

(1 mark)

10 Decide whether each of these sentences from the passage is **true** or **false** or whether you **can't tell**. Copy this table into your exercise book and complete it.

	true	false	can't tell
a) More people play and watch football than any other sport.			
b) People all over the world have heard of Beckham.			
c) The Brazilian footballer Ronaldo had an unhappy childhood.			
d) Football manager Bill Shankly thought people took football too seriously.			
e) Germany won the World Cup in 2002.			

(5 marks)

11 Write down a word from the passage which fits each of the following meanings:

a) a strong desire or aim in life

b) the area near where someone lives

84

c)   an ability or skill

d)   a sporting competition involving a series of events.

(4 marks)

Total – 25 marks

Taking a closer look

Paragraphs (2): topic sentences

Usually a paragraph will have a **topic sentence** – that is, a sentence which sums up what the whole paragraph is about.

Look at the first paragraph of the football passage. It begins with this sentence:

Soccer is the most popular sport on Earth.

The rest of the paragraph develops this idea:

It is played by millions of people around the world – on green fields, tropical beaches and dusty roads. It is played by the rich and the poor, the young and the old, by men and women of every colour, religion and background.

For practice

1 Here are some more paragraphs which talk about sports.

   a) Can you find the topic sentence in each one?

   b) Discuss how the rest of the paragraph picks up the idea in the topic sentence and takes it further for each one.

A Like most sports, tennis uses a number of specialist terms. Lob, overhead smash, ground stroke, let and fault are just some of the terms that players will become familiar with.

B Today badminton is played in more than seventy countries across the world. The history of badminton goes back many centuries. It is known that the game was played in some form in Ancient Egypt. It was also played in India in the nineteenth century and British army officers who were stationed there took an interest in it. When they returned home, they played at Badminton, the estate belonging to the Duke of Beaufort, which is how the game got its name. The rules of the modern game of badminton were decided on in 1887.

C There are three main types of golf club: woods, irons and putter. The woods are used for long-distance shots from the tee. The irons are of various types. The weight and the length of their shafts are different and the faces of the irons are set at different angles. Finally, the putter is used for hitting the ball into the hole on the green.

2 Now use one of the following topic sentences to start off a paragraph of your own. Write about four or five lines expanding on the idea contained in the topic sentence.

★ There are many different sporting activities available at our school.

★ I have some exciting plans for the summer holidays.

★ _____ is a hobby/activity I have always been very interested in.

Follow on

Topics for discussion

1 Do you support a football team? Make a list of reasons why you support it.

2 Conduct a survey in your class: what are the favourite sports? Discuss the reasons why you enjoy them.

For writing

1 Find out the facts about a sports star from football or from another sport of your choice. Write a short report on his/her life and career.

Follow on continued

FOLLOW ON WORK

2 Imagine you are a famous sports personality. Write about a day in your life.

Chapter 11

Tetra Pak

Have you ever wondered who invented the cartons used for milk and many other drinks?

Reading extract

1 When Ruben Rausing
presented a new idea for
packaging milk in 1952 many
people shook their heads in
5 disbelief. The invention,
which he named Tetra Pak,
looked like a miniature
pyramid and was made out of
paper. Some feared it would
10 leak; others said they would
much rather stick to glass bottles.

In spite of this resistance, Rausing did not give up.
Today his ideas are used all over the world. Since the
1950s, the Rausings have become one of the four richest
15 families in the world. They run an international company
producing some 30–40 billion units a year of packaging,
for milk, cream, soft drinks and even table wine.

Ruben Rausing's idea was that milk should be
packaged in a way similar to how sausage meat is
20 crammed into a skin. He invented a machine that
produced a long paper tube that could be cut off and

Reading extract continued

sealed at both ends after having been filled with milk.

His first model, the pyramid-shaped Tetra, soon became a hit. Shoppers found it lighter to carry than
25 traditional milk bottles. But it had a serious disadvantage – it was taking up too much space in the fridge. So Rausing went on to make a carton which looked like a small box with a spout. This model was easier to store, and is today the most common kind of packaging in many countries
30 throughout the world. In Europe, one out of two milk packages are made under licence from the Rausing empire. It has conquered a big market share in Asia and Australia, and can also be found in North America.

Ruben Rausing was not only a clever inventor. He
35 also understood how to run a successful business. He and his two sons, Gad and Hans, built up Tetra Pak as a family-owned group of some 40 companies, almost all of them in the packaging industry.

Though their products are well known, the Rausings
40 live a secluded life. They are wary of showing off their wealth and so try to avoid publicity, particularly
45 since an attempt was made to kidnap one of the family members
50 some years ago.

Questions

Section A

Complete these sentences by choosing the best ending from A, B or C.

1 When the Tetra Pak was first announced, some people:
- A thought it would not work
- B were amused by it
- C nodded in agreement

2 People did not like the invention at first because:
- A they thought it would not be suitable for holding liquids
- B it was made out of paper
- C they thought it was the wrong shape

3 The first type of Tetra Pak became popular because:
- A it did not take up as much space as a milk bottle
- B it could hold more than a bottle
- C it did not weigh as much as a bottle

4 The second type of Tetra Pak was even more popular because:
- A it was easier to pour
- B people preferred the shape
- C the shape was more convenient to store

5 'In Europe, one out of two milk packages are made under licence from the Rausing empire.' This means that:
- A half of Europe's milk production is controlled by the Rausing company
- B the Rausing company allows the design of their packaging to be used by other companies
- C half of European milk production is packaged by the Rausing company
                                                                  (5 marks)

Section B

1 Read paragraph four (lines 23–33).

   a) Write down one advantage of the original Tetra Pak design.

   b) Write down one disadvantage of the original Tetra Pak design. *(2 marks)*

2 Read paragraph five (lines 34–38).

   a) As well as being a clever inventor, what other skill did Ruben Rausing have? Answer **in your own words**
   (1 mark)

   b) Write down **ONE** piece of evidence that backs up your answer. *(1 mark)*

3 Read paragraph six (lines 39–51).

   a) **In your own words**, explain what is meant by 'the Rausings live a secluded life.' *(2 marks)*

   b) Write down the words from elsewhere in this paragraph that mean something similar to 'a secluded life'. *(1 mark)*

   c) Give **ONE** reason why the family prefers to live in this way. *(1 mark)*

Section C

4 Find a word from the passage that fits each of the following meanings:

   a) A smaller scale version of something (paragraph 1)

   b) a shape with sloping triangular sides (paragraph 1)

   c) opposition from people who do not agree with you (paragraph 2)

d) involving many different countries across the world (paragraph 2)

e) stuffed into a small space (paragraph 3)

f) the way things have always been done in the past (paragraph 4)

g) a large business which controls many smaller firms (paragraph 4)

h) cautious; not trusting people (paragraph 6) *(8 marks)*

Section D

5 Here is a summary of the passage. Fill in the gaps using **one word** or **two words** in each space. You may use your own words or words from the passage. Write your answers in a list, using the numbers given in each space.

The Tetra Pak is a method of packaging ____1____ which was first ____2____ to the public by ____3____ in 1952. It was made by ____4____ a paper tube through a machine that cut off and ____5____ both ends of the package. The original design was shaped like a ____6____ but later versions looked like a ____7____. This was so successful that it is now the most ____8____ method of packaging milk. The Tetra Pak is used throughout Europe, Asia, Australia and North America, making the Rausings one of the ____9____ families in the world.

(9 marks)

Total – 30 marks

Taking a closer look

Paragraphs (3): making links

In the last two chapters we saw:

- ★ how writers start a new paragraph when they move on to a new topic
- ★ how a topic sentence sums up what a paragraph is about.

Within a paragraph, a writer will often connect sentences and ideas together with joining words known as **conjunctions**.

The diagram below contains conjunctions that can be used to join sentences together.

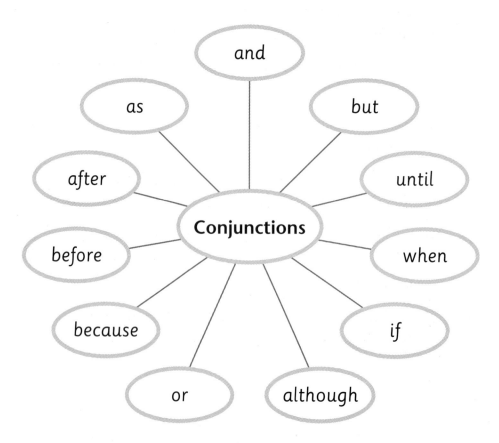

For practice

Pick a suitable conjunction to fill the gap in each of the following sentences.

1 Many people did not like the Tetra Pak _____ it first appeared.

2 _____ the Tetra Pak was invented, milk was usually supplied in glass bottles.

3 Rausing changed the original shape _____ the first Tetra Pak took up too much space.

4 Rausing kept experimenting with his designs _____ he came up with a successful product.

5 _____ the Tetra Pak was the Rausings' most successful idea, the family also built up 40 other companies.

6 Recycling is becoming easier _____ local councils are providing special bins.

7 Cans, newspapers, magazines, some plastics _____ glass bottles can all be recycled.

8 ___ more materials were recycled, the amount of waste that is buried in landfill sites could be cut down.

9 Only 10% of household waste is recycled at the moment ____ it would be possible to recycle about 50% of this material.

10 90% of household waste is either buried in landfill sites ___ burnt in incinerators.

Follow on

Topics for Discussion

Bring in **ONE** example of food packaging which you think works well. Show it to your class/group and explain why you think it is good.

Writing

The Rausings don't seem to enjoy being rich as they 'live in seclusion' and have had kidnap attempts.

1 Write about the good and bad things being rich would bring.

OR

2 Write a story based on a kidnap attempt.

Chapter 12

Teeth Braces

Today, many children have to wear braces on their teeth. The following passage looks at how this trend developed.

Reading extract

1   Teeth seem to be a never-ending source of discomfort
    for humans. Quite apart from the agony of toothache,
    and the dread of the dentist's drill, there is a whole
    world of problems in the way teeth grow. Too many
5   teeth, or teeth growing in odd positions in the jaw, is
    called malocclusion. This condition can cause anything
    from an unsightly smile to a swollen, deformed face.
        Adults are supposed to have 32 teeth, spaced
    regularly throughout the top and bottom jaw. They
10 should all be aligned in such a way that they fit
    together neatly when the jaw closes. Many of us are
    lucky enough to have such a set of teeth, but for those
    who don't, Norman W. Kingsley, an American dentist,
    invented in the late nineteenth century a branch of
15 dentistry called orthodontics. The word comes from the
    Greek *orthos* – straight and Latin *dens* – tooth.
        At this time, around 1880, the first modern teeth
    braces were designed. These applied a constant, mild
    pressure to the teeth, to gently change their position in
20 the jaw.

Reading extract continued

The first braces were ugly, unpleasant-looking devices. They had heavy metal plates which were anchored to teeth with dental cement, and clumsy thick wires connecting them together. Some braces

25   even had wiring that protruded from the mouth, and must have made the wearer feel very self-conscious. These days, braces are made of high-tech plastics and metals, some of which were developed by the NASA space programme. The wires that slowly pull the teeth

30   into position are stronger and more flexible, and are activated by body heat. Braces today are altogether more comfortable to wear. They also work more effectively, which cuts down on the time the patient has to wear them. For the daringly fashionable, some

35   braces are even available in bold, bright colours!

American dentists were the pioneers in this branch of dentistry, so it

40   seems fitting that America is the country where teeth braces are most common. Today, over four million American and Canadian

45   children (and even some adults) wear braces in any given year.

Questions

Section A

1 Find **ONE** word in the passage that means the same as each of these words or phrases.

a) not pleasing to look at (paragraph1)

b) not properly shaped (paragraph 1)

c) arranged in a straight line (paragraph 2)

d) department (paragraph 2)

e) stuck out (paragraph 4)

f) embarrassed (paragraph 4)

g) made to work (paragraph 4)

h) person getting medical treatment (paragraph 4)

i) first people to do something (paragraph 5)

(9 marks)

Section B

Complete these sentences by choosing the best ending.

1 'Malocclusion' is the name given to:
A   fear of dentists
B   overcrowded or wrongly positioned teeth
C   painful toothache

2 Teeth should be positioned so that:
A   top and bottom jaws are equal in size
B   top and bottom jaws can close together easily
C   top and bottom jaws can remain open

3 The branch of dentistry known as 'orthodontics' was first begun by:

   A an American dentist

   B a Greek dentist

   C a Latin dentist

4 Teeth braces work by:

   A heating the teeth

   B anchoring the teeth to the jaw

   C applying gentle pressure to the teeth   *(4 marks)*

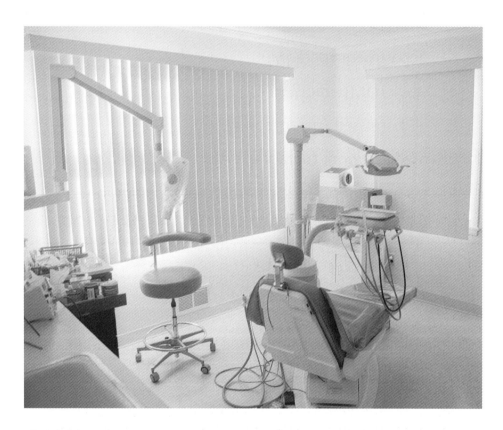

Section C

Look at these sentences about the second half of the passage (lines 21–47). Decide whether each sentence is **true** or **false** or whether you **can't tell** from the passage. Copy this table into your exercise book and complete it.

	true	false	can't tell
a) The earliest teeth braces were made of heavy dental cement.			
b) Materials developed by the NASA space programme are now used for teeth braces.			
c) Modern teeth braces are less expensive than the earlier ones.			
d) Most people now wear brightly coloured teeth braces.			
e) Teeth braces are only effective on children's teeth.			

(5 marks)

Section D

Here is a summary of the passage. Suggest **one word** or **two words** to fill each space. You may use your own words or words from the passage. Write your answers in a list, using the numbers given in the gaps.

Teeth cause people a great deal of ____1____. Toothache is very ____2____ to anyone suffering from it, and many people are ____3____ of going to the dentist. In addition, people may suffer from 'malocclusion', a condition caused by having too ____4____ teeth, or teeth which are wrongly ____5____ in the jaw. Orthodontics is the ____6____ of dentistry which can help this condition. Norman W. Kingsley was the American dentist who began orthodontics in the ____7____ century. Teeth braces work by applying gentle ____8____ to the teeth to move them into the correct position. The earliest braces were heavy and uncomfortable to ____9____, but modern braces are more effective and look better. Fashionable people sometimes even choose to wear

___10___ braces. Today, ___11___ is the country where teeth braces are most common, in both children and ___12___.

(12 marks)

Total – 30 marks

Taking a closer look

Describing Words

An **adjective** is a describing word. It tells you more about a thing or a person.

An **adverb** tells you **how, where** or **when** an action is done. Some adverbs can tell **how much**.

Most adverbs telling 'how' end in **–LY**. However, a few adjectives also end in **–LY**. Can you tell the difference?

For example: 'a friendly face' – 'friendly' describes 'face' and so it is an adjective.

Sita danced 'brilliantly': 'brilliantly' tells you how Sita danced – it is an adverb.

For practice (1)

Say whether the underlined words in these extracts adapted from the passage are adjectives or adverbs.

1 an <u>unsightly</u> smile

2 adults are supposed to have 32 teeth, spaced <u>regularly</u>

3 they fit together <u>neatly</u>

4 braces apply pressure to teeth, to <u>gently</u> change their position

5 the first braces were <u>ugly</u> devices

6 the wires <u>slowly</u> pull the teeth into position

7 modern braces work more <u>effectively</u> than earlier ones

For practice (2)

Think of a single word to fit each of these gaps and write it down. Then write down whether it is an **adjective** or an **adverb**.

1	My friend's sister is a very _____ girl.	adjective	adverb
2	David spoke very_____ as he was so excited.	adjective	adverb
3	The goal-keeper dived _____ for the ball.	adjective	adverb
4	My dog has _____ ears.	adjective	adverb
5	The audience clapped _____ when the band came on.	adjective	adverb

Follow on

Discussion

1 Think of **TWO** inventions which you think have made people's lives easier or more pleasant and write them down.

2 Compare your ideas with others in your class or group. Explain the reason for your choices.

Writing

1 Write an account of a visit you have made to the dentist or orthodontist. Try to describe how you felt about your visit – before, during and after.

Follow on continued

FOLLOW
ON
WORK

OR

2 'Fears'

Some people are afraid to go to the dentist. Write about any other things which you are afraid of, giving your reasons.

Chapter 13

Tourism in Majorca

Majorca, one of the Balearic Islands off the coast of Spain, is a popular tourist resort.

Reading extract

1   Majorca attracts about three million tourists a year. The capital, Palma de Majorca, has an airport 7 km to the east. There is also a busy ferry terminal. The island has hundreds of beaches and hotels, but it also has some spectacular and
5   remote scenery, such as the Sierra de Tramuntana, a ridge which provides superb walking country for those who are tired of the beaches. The economy of the island has been completely changed by tourism. The small-scale agriculture has all but disappeared.

10   Famous people have been coming to this island for hundreds of years. They came for the solitude and the wonderful climate. Majorca has warm winters and the sea is always there in the summer if you want to cool off. The writer Georges Sand and the composer Chopin

15   came here in the nineteenth century. And the English poet, Robert Graves, made his home in the village of Deia. He's buried there. In the 1960s, lots of hippies from the rest of Europe came here to live simply and cheaply.

20   'Tourism really took off about twenty-five years ago,' says hotel and bar owner Luis Torres. ' I've been living and working on the island since 1976. I opened a bar first of all. It did very well. It was close to the beach and hotels. It was always packed in the summer. At first I

25   didn't know how it would work out in the winter but there were still lots of tourists around. They tended to be older than the summer ones. They were retired and richer. They meant that my business could be kept going all year round and this made a big difference.

30   After five years I had made enough money to be able to open a small hotel.

The tourist trade has remained good to the island in spite of the recession. People still seem to be able to afford to come here.'

Questions

Section A

Choose the correct ending to each sentence from A, B or C.

1 The main purpose of paragraphs one and two is:
  A to discuss the importance of tourism to Majorca
  B to provide a history of the island
  C to give a list of famous people who have visited Majorca

2 The main purpose of paragraphs three and four is:
  A to describe how the tourist industry in Majorca started
  B to allow one hotel and bar owner to describe his own experience of running a business
  C to discuss whether people can afford to take holidays in Majorca

3 The biggest growth in the Majorcan tourist industry took place:
  A in the 1960s
  B in the 1970s
  C in the 19th century

4 The main reason for the success of Luis Torres' bar was that:
  A it was close to the beach
  B it was open in the winter
  C he was the first to open a bar on the island   *(4 marks)*

Section B

Answer these questions, **using your own words** where possible.

1 What **TWO** means of transport do visitors use to get to Majorca? *(2 marks)*

2 Write down **THREE** different attractions for tourists in Majorca. *(3 marks)*

3 **In your own words**, explain how tourism has changed the way the people of Majorca earn their living. *(2 marks)*

4 **In your own words**, explain **TWO** reasons why famous people came to visit Majorca in the past. *(2 marks)*

5 How can you tell that Robert Graves was particularly fond of Majorca? *(1 mark)*

6 Why did European visitors begin to flock to the island in the 1960s? *(1 mark)*

7 In the second paragraph the climate is described as 'wonderful'. From the first paragraph, find two other adjectives which also describe Majorca as being excellent in some way. *(2 marks)*

8 What worried Luis Torres when he first opened his bar? *(1 mark)*

9 What **TWO** differences did he notice between the summer and winter visitors? *(2 marks)*

Section C

Find a word from the passage to fit each of the following meanings:

a) working on the land, growing crops and keeping animals (paragraph one)

b) a long, narrow range of hills (paragraph one)

c) the organisation of business, money, industry, etc. in a country (paragraph one)

d) distant or far away (paragraph one)

e) a period when business is having difficulties, trade is slow and people are less well-off (paragraph four)   (5 marks)

Total: 25 marks

Taking a closer look

Fact and Opinion

In the first two paragraphs of the passage, the writer talks about the attractions of Majorca and about some of the people who visited the island in the past.

The writer gives us many **facts**. For example:

★ Majorca attracts about three million tourists a year.
★ The capital of Majorca is called Palma.

What other facts can you find in these paragraphs?

In the third and fourth paragraphs we get the viewpoint of one person in particular, the hotel owner Luis Torres. He gives his own **opinion** – another person might have had a different opinion.

The style of writing in this part of the passage is also different:

★ Personal pronouns are used, particularly 'I'.
★ Speech marks show that this is spoken, not written, English.

Here are some more statements about Spain. Make a list of them in two columns, one headed 'fact' and the other 'opinion'.

1   Spain is the second largest country in Western Europe.

2   The population of the capital city, Madrid, is five million.

3   Spain is the most enjoyable destination for a summer holiday.

4   Goya, El Greco, Salvador Dali and Picasso were all famous Spanish artists.

5   Pablo Picasso was a better painter than Salvador Dali.

6   King Philip II's palace, El Escorial, is the most beautiful building in the world.

7   The Balearic Islands are situated approximately 200 kilometres from the coast of the Spanish mainland.

8   The growth of holiday resorts has spoilt the Spanish coastline.

9   Bullfighting is a popular spectator sport in Spain.

10   Bullfighting should be banned.

Follow on

Topic for discussion

Where do you enjoy going for a holiday? Prepare an account of one holiday you have enjoyed.

You could do this in writing or in the form of a talk to your group or class.

Writing

Where in the world would you specially like to visit? Find out some information about this place and write a report on it. You could try using the Internet or your school or class library to find out facts about your chosen country.

Chapter 14

The Highland Clearances

The 'Clearances' is the name which was given to the cruel eviction of many Scottish people from their homes to make way for sheep farming.

Reading extract

1   From around 1760 onwards, many landowners in the
north of Scotland brought sheep onto their estates. In
winter, the sheep needed to graze in the shelter of the
valleys – where many people lived. As a result, families
5   were turned off their land and lost their homes. They
were left with no way of feeding themselves.

    Elizabeth Gordon, Countess of Sutherland, owned a
huge estate in Scotland. Like many landowners, she

Reading extract continued

10 usually lived in London and spoke no Gaelic. Her
husband was the Marquis of Stafford. The Staffords
were enormously wealthy. The income from their
estates brought them £300,000 each year. This would be
worth many millions of pounds today. The Staffords
15 owned two-thirds of the land in Sutherland. The
Marquis became the first Duke of Sutherland, and he is
remembered as a 'Great Improver'. Yet even today,
many people feel bitter that the 'improvements' forced
on the people did not make life better for everyone.

20 James Loch was the **factor** who ran the Staffords'
estates. He did not like the Highlanders, believing they
were lazy and dirty. He cleared the main glens in
Sutherland where many people lived. The Highlanders
were not given a choice. At least 10,000 people were
25 evicted from their homes between 1807 and 1821 –
which was almost half the population of Sutherland.

Patrick Sellar, a lawyer, was employed by the
Countess of Sutherland to collect rents, keep accounts
and make sure the tenants obeyed estate rules. Like
30 James Loch, Sellar looked down on the Highlanders.

In 1814, remembered as the year of the Burnings,
Sellar evicted tenants in Strathnaver. He gave orders to
burn the hill grazing areas so there would be no food
for the tenants' cattle and the people would have to go.
35 Buildings were burned to stop the people staying on
the land.

A witness called Donald Macleod wrote:

*I was present at the pulling down and burning of the
house of William Chisholm, in which was lying his wife's*

Note

Factor: *someone who looks after other people's property*

Reading extract continued

40   *mother, an old bedridden woman of near 100 years of age. I told Sellar of the poor old woman. He replied, 'The old witch has lived too long. Let her burn!' She died within five days.*

      Between 1762 and 1886, hundreds of Clearances
45   took place – from Shetland to Arran, and from Aberdeenshire to the Western isles. During the century of the Clearances, about 100,000 people left the Highlands and went to America.

Questions

Section A

Find **ONE** word in the passage that means the same as each of these expressions:

1   privately owned area of land (paragraph 1)

2   put out of one's home (paragraph 3)

3   people who rent homes or farms (paragraph 4)

4   person who sees something (paragraph 6)

5   unable to get out of bed because of weakness (paragraph 6)   *(5 marks)*

Section B

Look at these sentences about the passage. Decide whether each sentence is **true** or **false** or whether you **can't tell** from the passage. Copy this table into your exercise book and complete it.

	true	false	can't tell
a) Sheep farming became less popular with Scottish landowners after 1760.			
b) Elizabeth Gordon liked Scotland although she rarely visited it.			
c) Some people still feel anger today at what the Duke of Sutherland did to his tenants.			
d) Patrick Sellar took care that no one was harmed when the 'burnings' took place.			
e) People were put out of their homes in many areas throughout Scotland.			

(5 marks)

Section C

Complete these sentences by choosing the best ending.

1 Families were evicted from their homes because:
    A they could not feed themselves
    B the Countess of Sutherland could not understand their Gaelic speech
    C their land was required for sheep

2 The Staffords (Duke and Countess of Sutherland):
    A mainly lived on their estates in Scotland
    B mainly lived in London

> **C** spent half their time in Scotland, half in London

3 The Staffords' income of £300,000 per year would be:
> **A** worth much more in today's money
> **B** worth much less in today's money
> **C** worth about the same in today's money

4 The number of people evicted on the Duke of Sutherland's orders was:
> **A** almost half the population of the county of Sutherland
> **B** one hundred thousand
> **C** less than ten thousand

5 During the years 1762 – 1886, many of the people who were evicted from their homes:
> **A** went to America
> **B** went to Shetland
> **C** went to Arran   *(5 marks)*

Section D

Here is a summary of the passage. Suggest **one word** or **two words** to fill each space. You may use your own words or words from the passage. Write your answers in a list, using the numbers given in the gaps.

From around 1760, many landowners in the north of Scotland ____1____ tenants from their homes in the valleys to make way for ____2____ to graze. Among the worst of these were the Duke and Countess of ____3____, who were already ____4____ wealthy, earning more than £300,000 every ____5____. The memory of their actions still makes many people feel ____6____. The men the Duke and Countess employed to do the evictions, James Loch and Patrick Sellar, despised the ____7____ whom they had to put out of their homes. The year 1814 was known as the year of the ___8___ . In one incident, Patrick Sellar ordered a house to be burnt down, even though an old ___9___ woman was lying inside. She died less than ___10___ days later.

(10 marks)

Total – 25 marks

Taking a closer look

Writing to persuade

In Chapter 13, you looked at the difference between **fact** and **opinion**. In the passage on 'The Highland Clearances', the writer wants to get across his opinion that the Clearances were evil. This is known as '**bias**' which means 'leaning to one side'.

Writers may express their opinions *directly*. In the introduction, the evictions are described as 'cruel' which is an **opinion**. However, writers can also reveal their opinions indirectly by presenting **facts** in a certain way. This can influence or '**persuade**' the reader to think in a certain way.

For example, we are told in line 9 that the Countess of Sutherland 'spoke no Gaelic'. This **fact** is given to make the reader think badly of her because she had not bothered to learn the language of her tenants.

Fact / response / reason could be set out like this:

FACT: The Countess of Sutherland 'spoke no Gaelic'. (Paragraph 2)

RESPONSE: The Countess took no interest in her tenants. She was self-centred and did not care about them.

REASON: Since she had not tried to learn the Gaelic language, it shows she was not interested in Scottish ways even though she owned a huge estate in Scotland. She probably never spoke to any of her tenants.

For practice

Fill in your responses, and the reasons for them, to the following facts:

1 **FACT**: The Staffords were 'enormously wealthy' but had their tenants driven out to make way for sheep-farming which would make even more money for them. (Write your comment on the Staffords.)

2 **FACT**: James Loch believed the Highlanders were all 'lazy and dirty'. (Write your comment on James Loch.)

3 **FACT**: Patrick Sellar gave orders to burn the hill grazing areas and the buildings. (Write your comment on Patrick Sellar.)

4 **FACT**: Donald McLeod warned Patrick Sellar that there was an old bedridden woman in the house he was about to burn. (Write your comment on Donald McLeod.)

Follow on

Topics for discussion

The Staffords were very wealthy, but they were also greedy, selfish and cruel. However, other rich people have used their money to help others.

Follow on continued

FOLLOW ON WORK

If you were very rich, how would you use your money?

Writing

1 Imagine you are present at the burning of William Chisholm's house. Write the story of what happens.

OR

2 Use the Internet or an encyclopedia to find out about the County of Sutherland today. Write a short report on your findings.

MAC ALLASTER

Chapter 15

The Ship That Cried

Many people know of the sinking of the **Titanic** in 1911, when the great liner hit an iceberg. However another large ship, the **Derbyshire**, was wrecked in more recent times.

Reading extract

1 On 9th September 1980 a huge **bulk carrier**, the *Derbyshire*, disappeared during a **typhoon**. All 44 people on board were killed that day.

   The *Derbyshire* set sail from Quebec in Canada bound
5 for Kawasaki, Japan, on 11th July 1980. It was carrying over 158,000 tonnes of iron ore, loaded into seven of the ship's nine holds. On board were 42 officers and crew, and the wives of two of the officers.

   The ship was just four years old, yet had already had
10 its problems. Two men had been killed on its maiden voyage in an engine room explosion. Another man, Ronnie Kan, had left the ship at a port half-way through a voyage. He said he could no longer stand the way the ship 'cried'. In heavy weather the stress on the
15 ship would make its hull creak and groan, as if it were 'crying'.

   A few days out from Japan, the *Derbyshire* was hit by typhoon Orchid with winds of up to 90 **knots** causing

> *Note*
>
> **Bulk carrier:** *large cargo ship*
> **Typhoon:** *violent tropical storm*
> **Knots:** *sea miles per hour*

Reading extract continued

20 waves up to 30 metres high. But the *Derbyshire* should still have been all right. On the ship's bridge Captain Underhill, a skilled seaman, was in charge. Equipment on board would have given him constant updates on the weather. He would have known how to avoid the worst of the storm, and how to cope with what did hit the ship.

25 On 9th September the *Derbyshire* sent a message to its owners. The message ran, 'Vessel **hove to**; violent storm force 11.' No problems were reported. It was the last that was ever heard from the *Derbyshire*.

On the 14th of September relatives of the crew were
30 told the ship was lost. The next day a Japanese aircraft searching for signs of the ship spotted an oil slick 32 km north-east of the last reported position of the *Derbyshire*. A sample taken later proved the oil was from the *Derbyshire*.

35 On the 24h of October a Japanese tanker sighted and photographed a lifeboat from the *Derbyshire*. It was half

> Reading extract continued

flooded and there was no one on board. The boat looked like it had been ripped from the deck by the sea, not launched by the crew.

40   Perhaps the 'crying' that drove Ronnie Kan from the ship was a clue to the disaster. Perhaps the *Derbyshire* simply wasn't strong enough, and the crying sound was the hull flexing and bending beyond its capabilities until it finally broke up.

45   In 1996 a mini-submarine discovered the *Derbyshire* 4km down, lying on the bottom of the Pacific Ocean. An investigation was made. The chief scientist reported that it did not look like the ship had broken in half. He believed that, as typhoon Orchid hit the *Derbyshire*,
50 hatch covers over its hold had been blown in by the force of the storm. It would have been like 17 tonnes of explosive blowing up on the ship. The hold had taken in around 9,000 tonnes of water, and the ship had sunk. No SOS had ever been sent because of what he
55 called 'the pure speed of events'.

    Perhaps the full story will never be known. But it is a fact that since the *Derbyshire* was lost over 300 other bulk carriers have sunk. There are lessons to learn from the disastrous sinking of the Derbyshire, but no one is
60 quite sure what those lessons are yet.

> **Note**
>
> **Hove to:** *stopped sailing*

Questions

Section A

1 Find **ONE** word in the passage that means the same as each of these words or phrases.

   a) storage areas below deck in a ship (paragraph 2)

   b) first (paragraph 3)

   c) news (paragraph 4)

   d) patch of oil on the surface of the sea (paragraph 6)

   e) limits of what it could do (paragraph 8)

   f) enquiry (paragraph 9)

   g) opening in a ship's deck (paragraph 9)   *(7 marks)*

Section B

Complete these sentences by choosing the best ending.

1 The *Derbyshire* disappeared:
   A after it had been nearly two months at sea
   B four years after setting out from Canada
   C after being at sea a few days

2 Ronnie Kan left the *Derbyshire* because:
   A two men had been killed in an explosion
   B the weather was very stormy
   C the ship made strange noises

3 Captain Underhill of the *Derbyshire*:
   A was experienced enough to cope in a storm
   B did not have the equipment to cope in a storm
   C let the ship hit something in the storm

4 The message sent from the *Derbyshire* on 9th September:
   A reported the ship had been damaged
   B reported the ship was breaking up
   C reported the storm but no other problems

5 The lifeboat sighted by the Japanese tanker looked like it had been:
   A launched by the *Derbyshire*'s crew
   B torn off the *Derbyshire* by the sea
   C cut off by the *Derbyshire*'s crew

6 The investigation of the wreck of the *Derbyshire* in 1996 believed:
   A 17 tonnes of explosives had blown up on the ship
   B the ship had broken in half and then had sunk
   C the ship sank when the hatches blew in and the holds filled with water

7 The loss of the *Derbyshire*
   A has taught ship owners a lot about safety
   B has not taught ship owners about what makes ships sink
   C was the last disaster of its kind   *(7 marks)*

Section C

Look at these sentences about the passage. Decide whether each sentence is **true** or **false** or whether you **can't tell** from the passage. Copy this table into your exercise book and complete it.

	true	false	can't tell
a) There were no women on board the *Derbyshire*.			
b) The *Derbyshire* had been built in 1976.			
c) Tests proved the oil slick sighted by the Japanese plane on 14th September was from the *Derbyshire*.			
d) Bulk carriers like the *Derbyshire* are more likely to sink than other types of ship.			

(4 marks)

Section D

Here is a summary of the passage. Suggest **one word** or **two words** to fill each space. You may use your own words or words from the passage. Write your answers in a list, using the numbers given in the gaps.

In July 1980, the *Derbyshire* left from ____1____. It was only a few days from its destination in ____2____ when it was hit by a ____3____. A message was sent to the ship's ____4____ to say they were being delayed but reported no problems. About a week later, a Japanese plane noticed an ____5____. This was discovered to have come from the *Derbyshire*. The following month, a Japanese tanker sighted one of the ____6____ from the *Derbyshire*. It was half full of water and there were no ____7____ on board. The wreck of the *Derbyshire* was finally discovered by a ____8____ in 1996, lying 4 km down on the bottom of the Pacific Ocean. Although an ____9____ was held, no definite reason for the disaster was established. Over three hundred ___10___ have sunk since 1996, but no ____11____ have yet been learnt from the fate of the ___12___.

(12 marks)

Total – 30 marks

Taking a closer look

Dictionary and Thesaurus Work

Some words have only one meaning. An example from the passage would be 'lifeboat'. Other words may have several meanings, and can also act as different parts of speech.

For example, in the passage the word 'iron' in line 6 is an adjective, meaning 'containing iron'.

If you look up a **dictionary**, you will find several meanings for the word 'iron'.

iron: *(noun)*

1 an element, a common metal from which steel is made

2 a golf-club with an iron head

3 a flat-bottomed appliance that is heated and used for smoothing cloth

(adjective)
4 made of iron; very strong

(verb)
5 to smooth with an iron

For practice (1)

Use a dictionary to find as many meanings as possible for the following words. Start with the meaning it has in the passage:

★ board (line 3)
★ hold (line 51)

* stand (line 13)
* charge (line 21).

For practice (2)

A **thesaurus** is a type of dictionary which lists words which all have the same or similar meanings.

Using a thesaurus . . .

a) Find **THREE** other words with the same meaning as:
  * huge (line 1)
  * spotted (verb, line 32)

b) Find **TWO** other words with the same meaning as:
  * skilled (line 21)
  * violent (line 27)
  * problem (line 28)

c) Find **ONE** other word with the same meaning as:
  * equipment (line 21)
  * disappeared (line 2)
  * relatives (line 30)

Follow on

Topics for discussion

1 An 'omen' is a sign which people believe warns of bad luck. Look at the third paragraph of the passage (lines 9–16). What 'omens' might superstitious people think were warnings of the fate of the *Derbyshire*?

Follow on continued

2 Superstitions. The following is a list of things which are thought to be either lucky or unlucky. In your class or group, decide which are which. Do you know of any other signs of either bad or good luck? Then discuss how far you believe in these 'omens'.

★ a black cat crossing the road
★ the number 13
★ seeing a single magpie
★ breaking a mirror
★ finding a four-leafed clover
★ stepping on cracks on the pavement
★ walking under a ladder
★ opening an umbrella in the house

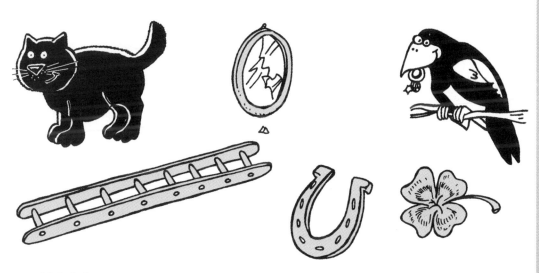

Writing

1 *'Storm at Sea'*

Write a short description of a ship in a storm. You may write as if you are looking at the scene from a distance or as if you are on the boat.

Follow on continued

OR

2 *'A Narrow Escape'*

Have you ever been in an accident or had a near-miss? Has anything frightening or dangerous ever happened to you? Write about what happened and try to explain how you felt at the time. If not, try to write about such an event from your imagination.

Chapter 16

Apollo 13

On 20th July, 1969, the first men went to the moon. In doing this, they achieved the goal of the 'Apollo' space programme run by NASA (National Aeronautics and Space Administration). The landing of the lunar module from Apollo 11 was an exciting moment for the astronauts, for the scientists at NASA who had made it possible, and for millions of people around the world who watched the event live on television. The problem for NASA and for America was what to do next.

Reading extract

1   NASA had enough government money to continue its programme of **lunar** exploration. It calculated that there were sufficient funds for nine more missions after Apollo 11. Apollo 12, which went to the moon in November
5   1969, and collected moon rocks, was a great success.

But the '60s were coming to an end, and some people's attitudes to space exploration were changing. An American flag now flew on the moon, so some people thought that the USA had already won the space
10   race. Others associated the moon programme with the politicians who had led the USA into an unpopular war in Vietnam, in South-east Asia.

> *Note*
> **Lunar:** *concerning the moon*

Reading extract continued

Even within NASA itself, some people felt that it was time to abandon moon exploration. Humans had been to the moon twice – what was the point of risking lives by sending further missions when there were other areas of space to explore? But in the face of such opposition, on 11 April 1970, Apollo 13 took off as planned.

At first everything went well. The launch was smooth, and for the first two days of the three-day journey to the moon the spacecraft worked perfectly. Then there was a loud bang, as one of the astronauts turned on a fan in the oxygen tanks.

A radio message was sent from the spacecraft: 'Okay, Houston; we've had a problem.'

They still had a problem, a big one. Although they did not know it yet, astronauts James Lovell, John Swigert and Fred Haise were facing a fight for their lives. Oxygen tank Number 2 had exploded when its fan was turned on. This had caused Apollo 13's other oxygen tank to burst its pipes and spill oxygen out of

35 the side of the spacecraft. Soon the command module was virtually useless, and the astronauts were forced to move through into the lunar module, named Aquarius, which should have been used for the moon landing. It was not designed to support three astronauts, and they had to use minimal power.

40 Low on oxygen and fuel, the astronauts nursed their spacecraft the rest of the way to the moon, around the lunar orbit and back towards earth. Once again, the drama of the space race caught the attention of millions of people. During the whole journey the world held its breath, waiting to see if the astronauts could

45 survive against all the odds aboard the ruined capsule. They did make it back safely, splashing down in the Pacific Ocean on 17 April 1970. NASA official Robert Gilruth said that Apollo 13 had been a frightening reminder that 'flying to the moon is not just a bus

50 ride.'

Reading extract continued

President Nixon visited NASA not long afterwards, awarding medals to the flight controllers who had helped save the Apollo 13 astronauts. But **the White House** had already let it be known that space was no
55 longer a national priority.

Note

The White House: *office and residence of the President of the USA*

Questions

Section A

Find **ONE** word in the passage that means the same as each of these words or phrases.

1 connected in thought (paragraph 2)

2 a separate unit in a spacecraft (paragraph 6)

3 as good as (paragraph 6)

4 the least possible (paragraph 6)

5 matter of first importance (paragraph 8) (5 marks)

Section B

Look at these sentences about the passage. Decide whether each sentence is **true** or **false** or whether you **can't tell** from

the passage. Copy this table into your exercise book and complete it.

	true	false	can't tell
a) The Apollo missions had to be cut back due to lack of funding.			
b) The moon rocks collected by the Apollo 12 mission were very valuable to science.			
c) The unpopular Vietnam war caused people to turn against the moon programme also.			
d) All the scientists at NASA thought the Apollo missions should continue.			
e) The astronauts did not realise at first how much danger they were in.			
f) President Nixon was sorry that the Apollo programme was not to continue.			

(6 marks)

Section C

Complete these sentences by choosing the best ending.

1 One reason why many Americans now turned against the Apollo moon missions was because:

    A the first two moon landings had not achieved very much

    B they felt America had already won the space race

    C they felt the money should be used for more useful things

2 Some NASA scientists, too, felt they should abandon the Apollo moon programme because:

135

    A the missions were too costly

    B they knew the public had lost interest in the moon

    C they wanted to explore new areas in space

3 The Apollo 13 mission:

    A operated perfectly for two days

    B seemed cursed by the number 13 from the start

    C was shocked by a loud bang as it was launched

4 The message 'Okay, Houston; We've had a problem' sent by the astronauts:

    A made the damage sound more serious than it was

    B made the damage sound less serious than it was

    C showed exactly how much damage there was

5 Millions of people took an interest in the return of Apollo 13 because:

    A they knew the astronauts were in great danger

    B the President was going to meet the astronauts

    C they knew it would be the last trip to the moon

(5 marks)

Section D

Here is a summary of the passage. Suggest **one word** or **two words** to fill each space. You may use your own words or words from the passage. Write your answers in a list, using the numbers given in the gaps.

There was great excitement when the Apollo 11 spacecraft first put men on the ____1____ in 1969. Later that year, men from the expedition known as Apollo 12 also landed and collected ____2____. However, public opinion turned ____3____ the Apollo space programme, and even NASA scientists thought there was little point in continuing with it. Nevertheless, in July 1970, the Apollo 13 mission was ____4____, and for two days everything went as planned.

However, a serious problem ____5____ when there was an explosion in one of the oxygen ____6____. The damage this caused meant all the astronauts had to go into the lunar ____7____, which was not designed to hold three men. However, they managed to ____8____ the spaceship around the moon and they finally ____9____ safely in the Pacific Ocean while millions of people watched anxiously. This helped people to realise how ____10____ the moon missions really were. Although some of those involved were awarded ____11____, the government made it clear the space programme was no longer considered a ____12____.

(12 marks)

Section E

1 Which part of the passage did the writer make most interesting for you?

2 Give a reason for your answer. *(2 marks)*

Total – 30 marks

Taking a closer look

Headlines

A **headline** is the title of an article in a newspaper or magazine. It will usually be in bold type (large black letters) to attract attention. Often there will be small headlines (known as **sub-headings**) in bold type at the top of some paragraphs as well.

A headline tries to capture the main idea in the article or in the paragraph it heads.

For practice (1)

Imagine you are a sub-editor in a newspaper. The *Apollo 13* passage will be printed and at the top of each paragraph you must put in a short '**sub-heading**' to show what it is about.

Your headline writers have given you the following suggestions. For each paragraph, select the sub-heading that you think best sums up the main topic of the paragraph.

You could do this exercise in groups.

Paragraph 1 (lines 1–5)
* ★ government money
* ★ moon rocks
* ★ Apollo programme continues

Paragraph 2 (lines 6–12)
* ★ attitudes are changing
* ★ flag on the moon
* ★ war in Vietnam

Paragraph 3 (lines 13–19)
* ★ abandon exploration
* ★ NASA say 'no point'
* ★ new areas of space

Paragraph 4 (lines 20–24)
* ★ 'we've had a problem'
* ★ a smooth launch
* ★ two good days

Paragraph 5 (lines 25–38)
* ★ forced to use lunar module
* ★ fighting for their lives
* ★ inside 'Aquarius'

Paragraph 6 (lines 39–50)
- ★ not just a bus-ride
- ★ the world holds its breath
- ★ safe splash-down

Paragraph 7 (lines 51–55)
- ★ medals for flight controllers
- ★ visit of the President
- ★ space no longer a priority.

For practice (2)

Now, choose a large headline to go over a newspaper article about Apollo 13 the day after it landed. In groups, discuss the following possibilities. Say why you think each of them would or would not make a good headline. Choose the one you like best, explaining why you have chosen it.

If you do not like any of them, your group might make up one of your own.

APOLLO SPACE PROGRAMME TO END

APOLLO 13 LANDS SAFELY IN PACIFIC

'HOUSTON, WE'VE HAD A PROBLEM!'

ASTRONAUTS FIGHT FOR THEIR LIVES

UNLUCKY 13 FOR THIRD MOON MISSION

PRESIDENT NIXON CONGRATULATES NASA

Follow on

Topics for discussion

1 Do you think the money spent on the Apollo space programme was worthwhile or a waste? Discuss reasons on both sides of the argument.

2 Danger: many people enjoyed watching the moon landings because of the danger involved. Suggest reasons why people enjoy doing dangerous things like mountain climbing or dangerous sports.

Writing

1 Imagine you are one of the astronauts on board Apollo 13. Describe your feelings after you hear the 'bang' and tell the story of what happens next.

2 Exploring space. What would you most like to learn about the universe outside our own planet?